My Tel Aviv Table

A journey of flavours and aromas from a sun-soaked city

LIMOR CHEN

NOURISH

EAT WELL, LIVE WELL

To Amir, Eldar and Daniella,
who fill my table with love and joy

MY TEL AVIV TABLE
LIMOR CHEN

First published in the UK and USA in 2023 by
Nourish, an imprint of Watkins Media Limited
Unit 11, Shepperton House, 83–93 Shepperton
Road, London N1 3DF

enquiries@nourishbooks.com

Publisher: Fiona Robertson
Commissioning Editor: Ella Chappell
Editorial support: Eldar Chen
Head of Design & Art Director: Karen Smith
Design Concept: Francesca Corsini
Commissioned Photography: Gareth Morgans
Food Stylist: Bianca Nice
Food Assistant: Charlotte Whatcott
Photography Assistant: Becci Hutchings
Prop Stylist: Hannah Wilkinson
Head of Production: Uzma Taj

A CIP record for this book is available from the
British Library
ISBN: 978-1-84899-417-1 (Hardback)
ISBN: 978-1-84899-418-8 (eBook)

10 9 8 7 6 5 4 3 2 1

Typeset in Poppins & Tangerine
Colour reproduction by Rivalcolour UK
Printed in China

Publisher's note
While every care has been taken in compiling
the recipes for this book, Watkins Media Limited,
or any other persons who have been involved
in working on this publication, cannot accept
responsibility for any errors or omissions,
inadvertent or not, that may be found in the
recipes or text, nor for any problems that may
arise as a result of preparing one of these
recipes. If you are pregnant or breastfeeding
or have any special dietary requirements or
medical conditions, it is advisable to consult
a medical professional before following any
of the recipes contained in this book.

NOTES ON THE RECIPES
Unless otherwise stated:
Use medium fruit and vegetables
Use medium (US large) organic or
    free-range eggs
Use fresh herbs, spices and chillies
Use granulated sugar (Americans can
    use ordinary granulated sugar when
    caster sugar is specified)
Do not mix metric, imperial and US cup
    measurements:
1 tsp = 5ml 1 tbsp = 15ml 1 cup = 240ml

nourishbooks.com

Contents

Welcome to Tel Aviv

Welcome to Tel Aviv

There is something special about Tel Aviv, a vibrant, young city built on the sands of the Mediterranean Sea, bustling with energy and full of life. With its late-night cafe culture and residents' love for outdoor living, the city has a unique buzz and beat. Enjoying warm weather almost year-round and the beach along its spine, you can't help but feel it's a city in constant holiday mode.

Unlike majestic and politically charged Jerusalem, Tel Aviv has the privilege of being the young, careless, hedonistic sister. Unencumbered by thousands of years of history and heritage, Tel Aviv is almost its own bubble. It is a melting pot of cultures mixing together in an adventurous, carefree manner.

The city never stops moving, never seems to sleep. Cafes are busy from early morning until late at night, often spilling onto the pavements. For a small city it offers such a huge variety of entertainment, from restaurants, clubs, bars and markets, to museums, concerts, theatres and galleries. I'm always amazed at how people manage to get to work the next day, as everyone is out and about until the small hours of the morning. It feels like we all live in the moment, making the most of everything that's on offer.

Food has a particularly important role in the city's life, and sometimes it feels that everything revolves around it. Food usually takes centre stage at the many festivals, Friday night dinners, Saturday lunches, family celebrations, picnics and barbecues. At the beach, before the theatre, after a concert – the social life of Tel Avivians is often centred around food.

It is a city made up of mostly immigrants from around the world who have brought their own twists on the food they grew up with, each family with its very own history of recipes, traditions and flavours. This has encouraged a culinary culture of experimentation, creativity and freedom of expression that is rarely seen anywhere else in the world.

Fast-forward a hundred years from its birth and Tel Aviv has now become a little culinary gem, renowned for its unique food and restaurant scene: a type of fusion cuisine influenced by the histories and cultures of its mixed population that utilizes the richness and abundance of the local produce.

Over the years, I began to appreciate more and more the place that my home city has in the culinary world. I remember while on holiday in Lisbon, we went to a well-known chef's restaurant. We loved the food – something in the dishes reminded me of home but I couldn't put my finger on it. On our way out, we met the chef who told us that he'd visited Tel Aviv and was so inspired by what he saw and tasted that his menu is now influenced by that food.

My Tel Aviv

I grew up in Tel Aviv and its suburbs. My childhood memories are entwined between the city and frequent visits to my grandmother's kibbutz (a socialist commune), Ashdot Yaakov, near the Sea of Galilee in the north of the country. It was the perfect combination of city life on the beach and countryside living, which I absolutely loved.

The beaches of Tel Aviv were both a focal point and a happy place for me. As a schoolgirl I used to meet friends there after school, usually at the "surfers" beach, where we would swim and surf or watch the sunset and enjoy ice cream, watermelon or cold drinks, bought at the little beach cafe.

This was my favourite hangout spot. Over the years, the little corner cafe we all loved evolved into a restaurant serving fresh grilled fish. And one by one more cafes and restaurants sprung up along the Tel Aviv shore. Today, there are endless restaurants dotted along the coast and I love that there is so much choice, from high-end to casual eateries, and many are enjoyed with your feet in the sand and a relaxed holiday feel. To this day, I love spending time by the beach; it's my preferred place to meet family, friends or just spend time on my own, reading, reflecting and connecting with nature.

I was always captivated by the architecture of the city, and how, in a strange way, it is influenced by the same factors that shaped the city's culinary scene. Eclectic-style buildings that were influenced by oriental and classical architecture, unique to the city, stand next to iconic Bauhaus buildings, of which Tel Aviv has the largest collection in the world, giving it the name "The White City" and protection as a UNESCO World Heritage Site. Largely designed by Jewish architects who left Germany during the rise of the Nazi regime and settled in Tel Aviv, they are immediately recognizable for their curved balconies, flat roofs, Crittall windows and minimalistic lines.

One street in particular means a lot to me: Bialik Street, named after Israel's national poet, who emigrated from Odessa and was invited by the city's mayor to live there. When Bialik died in 1934, his house became a museum, and at the entrance there is a large portrait of him painted by my maternal great grandfather, Haim Lifschitz, who was a well-known artist in the early 20th century. He knew Bialik from his time in Odessa, where they used to meet alongside other artists and thinkers. I love wandering around this area, thinking about my roots and the adventures and circumstances that led to my life in Tel Aviv.

At some point during my teenage years, my family relocated to London. The move shook me to the core. I longed for home and my life as it was, so decided to move back to Tel Aviv on my own. I studied at Tel Aviv University and loved living in the city, enjoying everything it had to offer. Yet life had its own plans and a few years later I married my childhood sweetheart, Amir, and moved with him to New York and then back to London.

From my family's table to yours

As with many other families in Israel, my parents came from completely different culinary backgrounds. My mum was born in Israel. Her father came from a family who had lived near the Sea of Galilee for six generations, originally from Eastern Europe, and her mum immigrated from Odessa in the 1920s. She grew up in a kibbutz, an agricultural commune, where all meals are taken in the communal dining hall. These were uncomplicated meals made from local produce: dairy, poultry and lots of vegetables and fruit. There is a richness to

home-grown produce; nothing ever tasted as wonderful as the very fresh avocados, bananas, dates and pecans I ate there as a child.

My father on the other hand emigrated to Israel as a young boy from Iran. Typical of the Israeli melting pot of cultures and traditions, my father introduced another dimension to my mother's cooking. While she was focused on the beauty and simplicity of the ingredients, he introduced her to the spices and herbs of his childhood. From Iran he brought a rich tradition of family food. He loved cooking and had a real flair for it, and I think that's what filtered through to me. His dishes were wonderfully fragrant, with lots of herbs – coriander, parsley, dill and mint – as well as more exotic ingredients, such as barberries and dried lime. I learnt from my dad how to combine sweet with sour, use dried fruit, work with an abundance of herbs and spices, and not be afraid to experiment and use my intuition.

My mum was always very aware of the health benefits of the food we consumed. I believe she was quite ahead of her time in that regard. In our kitchen, there were always discussions over the advantages of whole grains, cider vinegar, turmeric, ginger, raw honeycomb, nutritional yeast, etc. When I started cooking, that was always at the back of my mind. I wanted to find ways to cook with less sugar, more herbs, to fry less and swap ingredients with healthier substitutes that still had lots of flavour. I still remember my mother referring to certain ingredients as having "empty calories", meaning they have no nutritional value. Her health-consciousness was never extreme, but there was an underlying awareness of good nutrition. Most importantly, my mother, who was a teacher and always worked outside home, cooked delicious food using easy, quick recipes. When I became a mum, I began to appreciate these even more!

From home cook to executive chef

I've been making art for many years, primarily sculptures and large-scale installations, for exhibitions and commissions. I was happily immersed in my art after completing a Masters in Fine Arts when my husband, Amir, suggested we embark on a restaurant venture together, based on my cooking. He had caught the "hospitality bug" when he'd developed his previous business, a large chain of bakery-cafes across London. As crazy as it seemed at the time, the prospect excited me. I had no idea what this journey would bring, but I was energized by the adventure we were about to embark upon. I trusted Amir's business intuition and proven ability to bring an idea to fruition with great success. I was also excited by the prospect of being able to share my dishes and apply my creativity to a new venture, whether it be the presentation of the food, selection of the crockery or design of the interiors. The latter was particularly satisfying to me as an artist and prompted me to create some site-specific installations for the restaurants.

To test the water, we approached a renowned private members' club in London, Soho House, who agreed to let us run a week's residency showcasing a small menu of my dishes. The residency was exhilarating and petrifying at the same time. I had to work alongside a team of experienced chefs in a very large kitchen serving hundreds of guests each day. The energy and success of the residency left us with a taste for more, and several months later, we opened our first restaurant, Delamina EAST, in Shoreditch, followed a year and a half later by Delamina in Marylebone.

delamina

The restaurants are our babies, and the team has become our extended family. Many of those that joined us on day one are still with us seven years on. As chef-patron, my main focus is the creation of the menu, in which I find joy and satisfaction. I have the pleasure of working with two wonderful head chefs, with whom I meet regularly to develop the menu. They are very experienced and professional, and I love them both dearly.

The experience of applying my cooking style and ethos to the restaurants and reaching a wide audience is wonderful and empowering. Ingredients are grilled, roasted and marinated using the many herbs and spices that I grew up with. Just like cooking at home, I try to make the restaurant dishes as light and nutritious as possible, minimizing frying, saturated fat and sugar. We source our ingredients from suppliers who are passionate about the quality and provenance of their products, and I love the menu development process that each season brings. Our kitchens are stacked with an abundance of herbs, spices, nuts and seeds, which we use generously for marinades, sauces, seasoning and garnishing. Many of these ingredients are also included in our house cocktails, bringing the scents and flavours of our cuisine to our drinks. The Delaminas are known for their large variety of vegetable dishes, always a big component of a Tel Aviv-style meal. Alongside several meat, fish, brunch dishes and desserts, there seems to be a growing list of Delamina signature dishes that guests repeatedly ask for or recommend to others.

Our children, now young adults, are an integral part of our food journey and have an input into the dishes I make at home and in the restaurants. Our son Eldar is a big foodie and a natural in the kitchen. Our daughter Daniella has more of a sweet tooth and enjoys baking. The family is usually my first port of call when testing new dishes for the restaurant. We'll have a big dinner where I lay out the food that I'm trialling, and the whole family will give me feedback. It's a great sanity check before talking to the chefs.

I've highlighted a few key ingredients throughout the book. I use them in many of my recipes and find that they always lift any dish they touch. To me, they represent the flavours of the region and my culinary heritage. They are ingredients I love for their distinct taste, colour and aroma, and I can't imagine my kitchen without them. The dishes you will discover here are a personal journey through my recipe books. They were created over the years by trial and error, handed down through family generations, developed for the restaurants, or simply a result of being a mum and the main cook in the house. Like the food of Tel Aviv, they are a mix of traditional and new, simple and complex, east and west.

In a similar way to my art, I find that developing recipes is another form of creative expression. It provides genuine satisfaction when these dishes bring people together and make memorable moments of joy. Hopefully some of this finds its way into your home.

How to use this book

Here are few things you might find helpful when using this book. I have tried to ensure that the recipes do not require complex or tedious methods and do not need special expertise to make. They taste and look wonderful and can be made in any home kitchen. When possible, I offer quick and simple shortcuts.

Salt

I always use Fine Pink Himalayan Salt for its lower sodium content. If you use a different type of salt it may affect the taste, so I recommend starting with slightly less and adding more if needed.

Oils

I use extra virgin olive oil for salad dressings and drizzles, for its rich flavour and nutritional value. I swap to Extra Light Olive Oil when light cooking and baking, as it has a more delicate flavour. I choose Rapeseed/Canola Oil when frying and roasting at high temperatures, for its low saturated fat content and high smoke-point.

Substitutions

Trust your instincts and don't be afraid to make substitutions when you feel it makes sense. For example, it's perfectly fine to replace turkey breast with chicken or one white fish with another – just keep an eye on cooking times.

Special ingredients

All the more exotic ingredients such as barberries, dried lime, sumac, grape molasses, sour cherries, etc, can be found in Middle Eastern, Turkish and Iranian shops, and online. Sometimes they're stocked at big supermarkets.

Oven settings

The oven temperatures in my recipes are for a fan oven, as I find this setting best for even cooking. But please bear in mind that there could be some slight variations, as each oven is different.

Enjoy the process

Finally, enjoy the process. Start with a clean and tidy space, have all ingredients and equipment to hand, and put on your favourite music. Have a small bowl next to you so you can throw all the bits and pieces you need to discard into it, and another bowl with boiling water to chuck the dirty cutlery and dishes into as you go along. These tips make the whole process smoother and much easier to clean at the end.

2

Brunch & Dips

A spread of dips and small salads on the table

to scoop up with pitta bread is a typical way to start a meal in most areas of the Eastern Mediterranean and Middle East. Little vibrant plates are laid out in front of you, enticing you to taste them all, a plentiful selection of flavours and textures. Very quickly hands start passing the mezze across the table from one person to another like a dance: tearing, scooping, dipping and eating. A joyful and colourful medley.

Sharing mezze plates (or *mazetim* in Hebrew) is an exciting and generous way to start a meal; in addition to it being a culinary celebration, it's a social experience. To me, few things beat tearing a pitta, scooping up your choice of dip and enjoying all the flavours with friends and family. It feels like the essence of Middle Eastern hospitality, with all the warmth and happiness that food can bring.

You'll find some of my favourite dips in this section, from deliciously rich and healthy muhammara to zesty labneh, my mother's aubergine dip, aromatic tomatoes, spicy zhoug and of course my favourite, tahini. Most are a permanent feature both at home and on our Delamina menus. A good sourdough bread or fluffy pitta is a must to dip into the vast array of flavours and textures. I've also included a selection of my family's favourite brunch dishes and I hope you enjoy every bite as much as we do!

Shakshuka

Breakfast is king in Tel Aviv. It is such a lavish affair, with an assortment of dips, eggs, salads and breads spread across the table – yet the shakshuka takes pride of place as the crown jewel. Introduced by Jewish immigrants from North Africa, this dish has been lovingly adopted by Tel Avivians and become a cult classic. It's the most hearty and comforting dish, with eggs cracked right into the silky tomato sauce that holds so much flavour from all the vegetables, herbs and spices stirred into the mix. I love making a shakshuka on a lazy Sunday, sometimes making a green version, depending on what vegetables and herbs we have in our kitchen, although the classic tomato-based shakshuka remains my favourite. If I had to choose one dish for brunch, this would always be it.

SERVES: 2–4

1 onion, sliced

Splash of rapeseed/canola or vegetable oil

1 red pepper, deseeded and chopped into small cubes

2 medium-size plum tomatoes, chopped into small cubes

2 garlic cloves, diced

1 x 400g/14oz can of chopped tomatoes

½ tsp sweet paprika

½ tsp pul biber (Aleppo) chilli flakes

½ tsp sugar

½ tsp salt

4 eggs, depending on the size of your pan

30g/1oz feta cheese (optional)

To serve

Sumac

Pitta breads

In a large frying pan on a medium heat, sauté the onion in a splash of oil for 3–4 minutes until beginning to turn golden. Add the pepper and cook for a few minutes, mixing from time to time, until slightly charred.

Add the tomatoes and continue to cook for about 7–8 minutes until softened and slightly browned. Make sure you have enough oil so that the vegetables char rather than burn. This stage is important because it will give the depth of flavour. Mix occasionally; they will release a lovely aroma.

Once the onion, tomatoes and pepper have some colour, add the diced garlic, stir for about 1 minute, then add the canned tomatoes and mix well. Let everything cook for another 3–4 minutes.

Add the paprika, chilli flakes, sugar and salt. Mix until incorporated and cook for another 7–10 minutes. The sauce should reduce and thicken, turning a deep red colour.

Now create a little hole in the sauce with a spoon. Break an egg into that hole. Do the same with the rest of the eggs. Lower the heat, cover with the lid and cook for about 4–6 minutes, depending on how you like your eggs.

If you like, you can sprinkle crumbled feta cheese on top before serving. Sprinkle with sumac and enjoy with fluffy pitta breads.

Tahini

I've always had a love affair with tahini. To me, it's the queen of all dips and my all-time favourite. Everyone has their own preference, but I prefer mine to be slightly tangy. Tahini is so versatile and can be used in endless ways: as a dip with pitta, drizzled on top of roasted vegetables, as a salad dressing, as a sauce for falafel, with meat and fish and even as an ingredient in desserts. Tahini can be found everywhere in Tel Aviv, from street food to the trendiest and most refined restaurants.

SERVES: 2–4

100g/3½oz raw tahini

½ garlic clove, crushed and mashed into a smooth paste (optional)

7–8 tbsp water (add a couple more if needed)

2½–3 tbsp lemon juice

½ tsp salt

See page 32

Before starting, it's important to mix the tahini well and scrape from the bottom when mixing, as the oil always separates and stays on top.

Adding garlic is optional but if you do it's important to mash it to a paste, creating a smooth consistency instead of a bitty one. To make the paste, crush the garlic or chop it very small, add a tiny pinch of salt and then, using a knife, mash the garlic with the flat side of the blade. Keep mashing until it loosens up and becomes a smooth paste.

Place all the ingredients in a medium bowl and whisk together by hand, or mix with a fork, to a smooth and creamy consistency. Check the flavours and add a touch more lemon or salt if needed.

The tahini can be kept in the refrigerator, covered, for a few days. When using it, add a little bit of water to loosen it up.

Aubergine Dip

As soon as my mother covered the stovetop with foil, I knew we were in for a treat. She had begun the prep for her roasted aubergine/eggplant dip. Slowly our home would fill with the smoky smell of burnt aubergine skin and soon after we would enjoy its heavenly taste and soft meaty texture. Aubergine dip is vastly popular throughout the Middle East, with slightly different names and variations.

SERVES: 2–4

2 small-medium aubergines/
  eggplants (400g/14oz uncooked;
  340g/12oz cooked flesh)

1 tbsp lemon juice

2 tsp extra virgin olive oil

½ tsp salt

Pinch of coarse ground
  black pepper

To garnish

Extra virgin olive oil

Handful of chopped parsley

See page 33

If you have a gas hob/stovetop, cover it with foil as this can be a bit messy.

Turn the flame to medium-high and place an aubergine/eggplant directly over the flame, turning it every few minutes until all the skin is blackened and the flesh is soft and cooked through. This takes about 12 minutes each, depending on the size. Repeat with the other aubergine.

Alternatively, preheat the grill/broiler to high and place the aubergines directly under the grill in the oven, turning every few minutes until you achieve a similar result (about 20–30 minutes). Even better, lay them on the barbecue.

Remove the aubergines from the heat and let them cool.

Peel the skin carefully, although it's okay if a few black bits remain. Chop the smoky aubergine flesh finely and transfer to a medium bowl.

Add the rest of the ingredients and mix well. Taste and add a bit more salt or pepper, if needed.

Drizzle over a little extra virgin olive oil and sprinkle with chopped parsley to garnish, and it's ready to scoop.

Spicy Tahini

This spicy tahini recipe is perfect for when you want to give a dish a bit of a kick. I like to use pul biber (Aleppo) chilli flakes, as they're mild and allow me to control the heat, while also turning the tahini a vivid pink/orange colour. If you prefer it spicier, you can increase the amount of pul biber, with the colour deepening the more you add. If you decide to use regular chilli flakes, then halve the amount. Always start with less (it can take time for the flavour to develop); you can always add more.

SERVES: 2–4

100g/3½oz raw tahini

1½ tsp pul biber (Aleppo) chilli flakes

10g/¼oz/⅓ cup parsley, finely chopped

2½ tbsp lemon juice

6 tbsp water

½ tsp salt

See page 33

Mix all the ingredients together in a bowl until well combined.

Set aside for at least 30 minutes before serving until the chilli infuses the tahini. Mix well; it will turn slightly pinkish and then is ready to eat.

Zhoug

Tel Aviv was introduced to this spicy and herby green dip as a result of immigration from Yemen in the early 20th century. It's the go-to dip when looking for added heat, and you won't find a street-food stall without it. The level of chilli varies, but in some places it can have a really strong kick. It's great as a topping for hummus and tahini, and goes well with a variety of meats. This recipe, which is also used in our Delamina restaurants, is medium-hot, but you can adjust it to your personal palette.

SERVES: 2–4

2 small garlic cloves, crushed and mashed into a smooth paste

3 medium-strength green chillies, deseeded and finely sliced

70g/2½oz/3 cups coriander/cilantro, washed and chopped

½ tsp salt

¾ tsp ground cumin

2 tbsp/25ml water

3 tbsp/45g olive oil

See page 32

To make the garlic paste, see page 30.

Place all the ingredients into a food processor and blitz until almost smooth. (This has a similar texture to chimichurri.)

Muhammara

Roasted Red Pepper, Walnut & Pecan Dip

Muhammara is perhaps not as iconic as hummus and tahini, but what it lacks in fame it compensates for in flavour. Its origins lie in Syria, and it has now become popular throughout the whole region. This terracotta-coloured dip can accompany any meal or can be enjoyed as a starter on its own, to be scooped with a fluffy pitta or spread on bread. It has a deep and rich flavour derived from the roasted red peppers, which marry wonderfully with earthy walnuts and pecans. Along with the touch of acidity and sweetness from the pomegranate molasses, the ingredients balance each other in beautiful harmony. The striking reddish colour coupled with these nutritious ingredients makes it a standout dip for me.

SERVES: 6–8

30g/1oz roasted walnuts

30g/1oz pecans

30g/1oz/⅓ cup breadcrumbs

1 tbsp lemon juice

2 tbsp pomegranate molasses

1 small garlic clove, chopped

80ml/2¾fl oz/⅓ cup water
  (including some of the
  liquid that comes out of
  the roasted peppers)

1 tsp salt

½ tsp ground cumin

½ tsp sweet paprika

2 tsp pul biber (Aleppo) chilli flakes

2½ tbsp olive oil

2½ tbsp rapeseed/canola oil

To make the roasted red peppers

3 whole red peppers

1 tbsp olive oil

Pinch of salt

Pinch of freshly ground
  black pepper

To garnish

Drizzle of olive oil

A few chopped roasted walnuts

Mint leaves

Preheat the oven to 220°C/425°F/Gas 7.

First, make the roasted red peppers. In a baking pan, coat the peppers with the olive oil and season with the salt and pepper. Roast in the oven for about 30–40 minutes, turning halfway through. During that time, they should char nicely.

Carefully transfer the peppers into a heatproof bowl and cover. Leave for about 15 minutes to let them steam and cool down. Some liquid will come out. Keep it. It's full of flavour and you want to use it later.

Scatter the walnuts and pecans on a baking tray and roast in the oven for about 10 minutes. It may not look like they change much, but it makes all the difference. Do not burn them, as they will become bitter and alter the flavour of the dip completely.

Take the peppers and pull off the little stem at the top. Slice them open and discard the inside with all the small seeds. Peel the skin off until you have only the flesh. Discard the skin. Slice the peppers into strips.

Put the red pepper strips into a food processor and start adding all the other ingredients, adding the oils last by pouring slowly. Blitz until slightly grainy.

Spoon onto a serving bowl and garnish with a drizzle of olive oil, the chopped walnuts and a few mint leaves.

Roasted Tomato Spread

Apparently as a child I was an extremely picky eater and liked very few foods. But the one thing I loved and ate more than anything else was tomatoes. According to my parents, I grew up eating tomatoes and devouring them in any shape or form, something that has been passed down to my daughter Daniella. So, it's no surprise that I had to create a tomato spread for Delamina, and it has been on the menu from the beginning. This one has an irresistibly intense depth of flavour that I hope you'll enjoy.

SERVES: 2–4

6–8 tbsp olive oil

3 large tomatoes, sliced into discs or thin wedges

2 garlic cloves, crushed

½ tsp pul biber (Aleppo) chilli flakes

Pinch of salt

To serve

Sourdough bread

To garnish

Pinch of pul biber (Aleppo) chilli flakes

Chopped parsley

See page 38

Place a large frying pan on a medium heat, pour in 3–4 tablespoons of the olive oil and let it heat up. Add the tomatoes in one layer so they cover the whole pan. If you need to, do this in batches, but it's important that they don't overlap.

Let the tomatoes cook for a few minutes without moving them. Add the crushed garlic, chilli flakes and salt and leave for a few more minutes until the tomatoes have softened completely.

Mash the tomatoes with a fork to make a paste-like consistency and cook for a few more minutes. Check the flavour and add a touch more salt, if needed.

Toast some sourdough bread. Spread the bread with a drizzle of the remaining olive oil. Spoon a generous amount of the tomato mix on the toast, drizzle with some more olive oil, then sprinkle with a pinch of pul biber and some chopped parsley. Eat while warm.

Butter Beans, Herbs & Urfa Chilli

This salad works well as a snack on its own or as an addition to any spread of dips and salads. The gentle heat from the urfa chilli goes so well with the soft and creamy butter/lima beans. A good-quality extra virgin olive oil helps elevate the dish even more.

SERVES: 4

400g/14oz/2 cups dried butter/lima beans, soaked in water overnight, then drained or 2 x 400g/14oz cans of butter beans, drained and rinsed

Handful of roughly chopped coriander/cilantro (no tough stalks)

1 tsp salt

½ tsp sweet paprika

1 tsp urfa chilli flakes

2½ tbsp lemon juice

2 tbsp extra virgin olive oil

See page 39

If using dry beans, put them in a small pan on a high heat, cover with boiling water (about 800ml/28fl oz/ scant 3½ cups) and bring to the boil. Simmer and cook with a pinch of salt for 1 hour until soft with a creamy texture. If you're using canned beans, you can skip this step.

Place the beans in a large bowl. Add the chopped coriander/cilantro and mix to combine.

Add the salt, paprika, chilli flakes, lemon juice and extra virgin olive oil. Mix it all together.

This is the kind of salad that will taste even better if made a day in advance.

Persian-style Omelette

My father was an omelette expert who would cook this dish for us frequently as kids, and my children would lap this up when I made it for them on weekends! The abundance of herbs and the turmeric help make it really nutritious as well as delicious. With its striking green and yellow colours, it makes a wonderful centrepiece for a healthy brunch when you want to whip something up quickly. It's also lovely with a dollop of yogurt on the side.

SERVES: 2–4

4 eggs

½ small onion, chopped very small

Handful of chopped parsley

Handful of chopped coriander/
  cilantro

Handful of chopped dill

½ tsp ground turmeric

¼ tsp salt

2 tbsp rapeseed/canola
  or vegetable oil

Dollop of plain yogurt (optional)

In a medium-size bowl, whisk the eggs with a fork.

Add the onion, herbs, turmeric and salt and mix well until combined.

Place a large frying pan on a medium-high heat and add the oil. When the oil is hot, pour in the eggs and reduce the heat, as we don't want the bottom to burn. Cover and let it cook fully, or flip it over after a couple of minutes when it has firmed up.

Transfer to a large plate and slice to portion. Serve with a dollop of yogurt, if you like.

Turkish-style Eggs with Urfa Chillies & Yogurt

This is my favourite way to eat poached eggs. I've given it my own twist, using urfa chilli alongside paprika for a mildly hot but sweet flavour, complemented by the garlicky yogurt.

SERVES: 4

½ small garlic clove, crushed and mashed into a smooth paste

400g/14oz/1½ cups plain yogurt

2 pinches of salt

2 tbsp white wine vinegar

4 eggs

20g/¾oz butter (about 1 tbsp)

5 tbsp olive oil

1 tsp sweet paprika

1 tsp urfa chilli flakes

A few dill sprigs, to garnish

Pitta breads or other bread, to serve

To make the garlic paste, see page 30.

Mix the yogurt with a pinch of salt and the garlic paste and set aside. There should be just a hint of garlic to the yogurt.

Take four plates, spread a couple of spoonfuls of the yogurt in a circular motion onto each plate, then set aside at room temperature.

For the poached eggs, place a medium saucepan with water on a high heat and bring to the boil, then reduce the heat to a simmer. Add the vinegar. Crack an egg into a small bowl first, as this helps to slide the egg into the saucepan.

Stir the water to create a whirlpool and drop the egg gently into the middle. When poaching more than one egg, slide them in one after the other from the side. For a runny yolk, take the egg out with a slotted spoon after 5 minutes, or leave a bit longer, depending on how soft you like your eggs. If you're making the poached eggs one at a time, place the cooked eggs in a bowl of lukewarm water to keep warm until all the eggs are ready.

When all the eggs are ready, take them out with slotted spoon, dab dry with paper towels and place one on each plate.

In a shallow frying pan, heat the butter and olive oil on a low heat, add a pinch of salt, the paprika and chilli flakes, then stir for a minute or two.

Take off the heat and drizzle the hot sauce in a circular motion over the yogurt and the eggs, a couple of spoonfuls each. Garnish with the dill. Scoop with fluffy pitta or any bread you like and enjoy.

Green Omelette with Leek, Kale & Barberries

During a video call with my sister Shelley, I noticed her son (my nephew) devouring this green omelette. Between his mouthfuls, he would explain how much he loves it, which was made clear by how quickly it disappeared! My sister revealed that this dish is a sneaky tactic to get him to eat more green veggies. But he's not the only one that loves it – I've since been making it for years, adding barberries to give it a slightly tangy edge. For some funny context, my nephew asked to have shrimp for his seventh birthday, so don't be fooled into thinking that this is a kids' recipe!

SERVES: 2–4

2 leeks, cleaned

15g/½oz/1 cup kale leaves, thick stems removed

2 tbsp dried barberries

3 tbsp rapeseed/canola or vegetable oil

4 eggs

¼ tsp salt

Pinch of coarse ground black pepper

¼ tsp sweet paprika

Slice the leeks lengthways and slice again into semi-circles (about 5mm/¼in thick).

Blanch the kale in a bowl of boiling water for about 3 minutes. Drain, squeeze the water out and finely chop.

Blanch the barberries (as above) for about 3 minutes, drain and keep aside.

In a medium-size shallow frying pan on a medium heat, heat the oil for a few seconds, then add the leeks. Sauté the leeks for about 3 minutes, stirring occasionally, and when they start to turn golden brown (or lighter if you prefer them less caramelized), add the kale and stir and cook for a few more minutes. Add the barberries, reduce the heat to low and mix it all together. Spread the mixture evenly in the pan.

Beat the eggs in a bowl and add the salt and pepper.

Pour the eggs evenly over the sautéed greens and barberries, sprinkle with the paprika, then cover the pan. Leave to cook through for about 4–5 minutes.

Sumac

Sumac is the spice I probably use the most. I adore its tangy flavour and I think almost every dish tastes better with a sprinkle of this burgundy-coloured wonder. It is definitely the signature spice of the Delaminas. Sumac goes spectacularly well with most dips, salads, rice and fish dishes. It's made of dried, crushed berries cultivated primarily in Turkey and Iran, and has a coarse texture. It's my best friend in the kitchen and you'll see it in many of my recipes.

Spiced, Rolled Labneh

A staple in the Middle East, labneh is a must-have in our household, mainly because my daughter and I can eat it all day long, usually with extra virgin olive oil and a sprinkle of sumac, spread onto sourdough, pitta or crackers. I'm always amazed by how easy it is to make and how wonderful it tastes! The spread is usually ready after 24 hours in the refrigerator (depending on the yogurt). If you leave it for 48 hours, it gets thicker and you can create these irresistible labneh balls in various flavours. Place the balls in an airtight jar and they can last for up to four weeks in the refrigerator. Don't worry if the oil solidifies, it will turn into liquid again after it sits at room temperature.

MAKES: 16–18 balls

500g/1lb 2oz/2 cups plain yogurt

½ tsp salt

2 tbsp za'atar

2 tbsp sumac

3 tsp pul biber (Aleppo) chilli flakes

3 tsp sweet paprika

Extra virgin olive oil

Place the yogurt in a medium-size bowl, sprinkle with the salt and mix well. Take a muslin cloth/cheesecloth or clean, thin cotton kitchen towel and spoon the yogurt into the middle, tying the four corners together.

Place the muslin in a sieve/fine-mesh strainer, then the sieve inside a large bowl, making sure there is a big enough gap between the sieve and the bottom of the bowl for the water to drip out. Place the bowl in the refrigerator. Discard the excess water after about 3 hours, then return to the refrigerator for 48 hours, checking occasionally, discarding the water if needed.

Take three flat plates and sprinkle the za'atar on one, the sumac on the second and the pul biber and paprika mixed together on the third.

Place a little bowl with oil next to you, so you can dip your fingers and palms in; otherwise they get sticky.

You can use one large jar and mix the flavours up or three smaller ones to keep them separate. Either way, sterilize the jar or jars before you start (see page 210).

Using a spoon, take the desired amount of labneh from the bowl, roll it between your oily palms to make a ball, smaller than a ping pong ball, then roll on the plate with the chosen flavour until it's completely covered and place the ball inside the jar. Repeat.

Once the jar is full, pour olive oil over the labneh balls until they are covered. They will last for 3–4 weeks in the refrigerator. The olive oil can be used again and again for other batches or as a salad dressing.

Granola with Yogurt & Sweet Tahini & Date Molasses Drizzle

Granola can be eaten any time of the day. This one is my preferred mix, but you can use other nuts like cashews or walnuts, as well as other berries to match your taste. I find this combination well balanced and fresh, with the tahini and date drizzle giving it a deeper and richer flavour.

MAKES: 10–12 portions

200g/7oz/scant 1 cup rolled oats

40g/1½oz/¼ cup pumpkin seeds

40g/1½oz/¼ cup sunflower seeds

40g/1½oz/⅓ cup pecans

40g/1½oz/⅓ cup almonds
  (with skin)

4 tbsp maple syrup

1 tbsp date molasses

For the tahini and date
  molasses drizzle

2 tbsp raw tahini

2 tbsp water

3½ tsp date molasses

To serve

400g/14oz/1⅔ cups plain yogurt

120g/4¼oz/scant 1 cup blueberries

120g/4¼oz/scant 1 cup raspberries

Preheat the oven to 170ºC/325ºF/Gas 3.

To make the granola, place the oats, seeds and nuts in a large bowl. Add the maple syrup and date molasses and mix well until combined and all the ingredients are coated in the syrup.

Spread the mixture out evenly on a large baking pan lined with parchment paper. Bake in the oven for 30 minutes with a timer set to stir the granola every 10 minutes. It's important to ensure it roasts evenly.

Take it out and let it cool. Once cooled down, transfer to an airtight jar and it will last a few weeks.

To make the drizzle, in a small bowl, mix the tahini and water first to dilute the raw tahini, then add the date molasses and whisk to a creamy texture.

For each serving, place 3–4 spoonfuls of yogurt in a small bowl, sprinkle with some granola, add some fresh berries and top with a little tahini and date drizzle.

Cheese & Za'atar Mini Buns

If you feel like adding some cheesy baked goodies to your brunch that are very quick to make, these will do the trick! The yogurt makes them light and airy with a slight tang, and you should get a crispy outside with a warm centre. They are irresistible straight from the oven, so although this recipe will make 10–12 buns, it might be worth doubling it! If you make them in advance, warm them in the oven for 5–7 minutes just before eating and it will be like they're freshly baked.

MAKES: 10–12 buns

4 heaped tbsp (110ml/3¾fl oz/ scant ½ cup) plain yogurt

3 heaped tbsp (100ml/3½fl oz/ scant ½ cup) cream cheese

70g/2½oz/½ cup grated mature Cheddar cheese

70g/2½oz/½ cup self-raising/ self-rising flour

50g/1¾oz/½ cup ground almonds

½ tsp salt

1½ tsp za'atar, plus 1 tsp to sprinkle on top

1 egg

1 tsp nigella seeds

Preheat the oven to 180ºC/350ºF/Gas 4.

In a large bowl, mix together the yogurt and cream cheese. Add the grated Cheddar, the flour, ground almonds, salt and za'atar and mix again.

Line a baking tray with baking parchment. Wet your hands, take a spoonful of the mixture and roll it into a ball. Place on the lined baking tray and press it a little to flatten out. Repeat with the rest of the mixture.

Beat the egg in a small bowl and brush it over the buns, then sprinkle with a little more za'atar and the nigella seeds.

Bake in the oven for 25 minutes until they are golden. Serve warm.

Vegetables & Salads

Vegetables have always been

a significant part of my cuisine and that of Tel Aviv, with seasonality playing a major role in the choice of ingredients. Years ago, when our country was still very young, our diet consisted predominantly of locally sourced fruit and vegetables. You could always tell what time of year it was by looking at the grocery shop window, and for me there was something comforting and reassuring in being tuned to nature and its cyclical rhythm.

I had the privilege of experiencing the seasons somewhat closely during my frequent and treasured visits to my grandmother's kibbutz. I learnt the beauty of waiting for the dates to be visibly ripe and ready to eat, or knowing when the pecans are in season, and have fallen from the tall trees and are therefore ready to be picked up, cracked and eaten. Being surrounded by farmland, strolling in banana plantations, visiting the dairy barn, as well as celebrating the annual harvest festival, Shavuot, all made me fully appreciate everything that nature offers, as well as the intensity of the flavour and the nutritional benefits of locally sourced ingredients.

It was therefore particularly strange to see oranges and watermelons side by side in the middle of July when I first arrived in the UK. Almost everything your heart desired was readily available year round, transported from the other side of the world.

Back home, we always had a plate of sliced vegetables with meals, such as tomatoes, radishes or cucumbers. It was something that both my parents grew up with and were accustomed to. My children grew up eating chopped salads with almost every meal and loved scooping up the tiny veg with a teaspoon. Their friends enjoyed it too – even the ones who didn't usually eat veggies at home (to their mothers' delight).

At Delamina, we are known for our varied and flavoursome vegetable dishes that change with the seasons. We serve daily specials that celebrate ingredients that are hyper-seasonal and local. In this section, you'll find a wide selection of vegetable dishes, from a variety of salads to quiches, fresh and cooked, sides and mains. It is the largest section of my book, reflecting my love and passion for vegetables.

Fig, Roasted Goat's Cheese & Hazelnut Salad

If only figs were in season all year round! They have such a unique texture and a lovely sweet flavour, so I always try to make the most of them during their short season. This can mean either basing a dish around them or using their flavour to transform a recipe. This salad is an example of the former. Figs are one of the staple fruits in the region, going all the way back to biblical times. They are actually one of Israel's "seven species" that symbolize the prosperity of the land, along with olives, pomegranates, dates, grapes, wheat and barley.

SERVES: 4

30g/1oz hazelnuts

1 tbsp olive oil

¼ tsp garlic salt

200g/7oz goat's cheese, sliced into discs approx. 1cm/½in thick

100g/3½oz frisée

2 endives

6 figs, cut into quarters

Dressing

1 tsp smooth Dijon mustard

1 tbsp whipping cream

1½ tbsp extra virgin olive oil

1 tsp honey

2 tsp lemon juice

Pinch of pul biber (Aleppo) chilli flakes

Pinch of pink Himalayan salt

See page 60

Preheat the oven to 200ºC/400ºF/Gas 6.

Put the hazelnuts in a bowl and sprinkle with the olive oil and garlic salt. Mix well and spread out on a baking tray. Roast in the oven for 10–12 minutes until golden. Take out and leave to cool.

Turn the oven to the grill/broiler setting at 220ºC/425ºF. Put the goat's cheese slices under the grill for a few minutes until the tops are golden and have slightly melted. If using a large log of goat's cheese, let them cool a little and then slice each circle into 4 triangles.

Wash the lettuce and endives well, dry and place on a large, flat salad plate (better than a bowl).

To make the dressing, mix the mustard and cream together in a small bowl, then add the olive oil, honey, lemon juice, pul biber and salt and mix well.

Drizzle a few spoonfuls of the dressing onto the leaves and toss, then place the figs and goat's cheese on top and sprinkle over the roasted hazelnuts. Drizzle with more dressing and serve.

Baby Kale & Candy Beetroot Salad with Cashew & Za'atar Crumbs

When we were growing up, my mum instilled in me and my sisters the importance of good nutrition. This has stayed with me when preparing food, but never at the expense of taste. There is no reason why nutritional meals cannot be delicious to the mind, body and soul. I wanted to make this kale salad colourful and enticing, but not complicated, with interesting textures and flavours. It was a very popular salad at Delamina; I hope you agree!

SERVES: 4

12 mini plum tomatoes or other cherry tomatoes, cut in half lengthways

½ tsp salt, plus extra for seasoning

½ tsp soft brown sugar

2 medium beetroots/beets (I recommend the candy variety), cut into eighths or smaller wedges; they should be bite-size and not too big

2 tsp maple syrup

1 tbsp olive oil

300g/10½oz/4 cups baby kale (or regular kale works fine)

2 yellow carrots, peeled, thinly sliced

For the breadcrumbs

1 large slice of sourdough bread (about 40g/1½oz)

40g/1½oz/scant ⅓ cup cashews, crushed

1 tbsp chopped parsley

2 tsp za'atar

2 tbsp extra virgin olive oil

For the dressing

1 tbsp lemon juice

1½ tsp sherry vinegar

2 tbsp walnut oil

1 tsp black grape molasses

½ tsp soft brown sugar

Pinch of salt

Pinch of freshly ground black pepper

See page 61

Preheat the oven to 140°C/275°F/Gas 1 and line a baking tray with baking parchment. Spread out the tomatoes on the lined baking tray and sprinkle with the salt and sugar. Bake in the oven for 30 minutes, until they become semi-dry.

Turn the oven up to 180°C/350°F/Gas 4. Put the beetroots/beets in a baking pan and season with salt, the maple syrup and olive oil. Cover with foil and cook in the oven for 1 hour. Uncover and cook for a further 30 minutes. (For a shortcut, you can use ready-cooked beetroot, but ensure it is not in vinegar. Cut and season as above and cook uncovered for 20 minutes.)

Meanwhile, make the breadcrumbs. Tear the sourdough into a food processor and blitz until it becomes crumbs. Add the cashews and blitz for a minute. Transfer the mixture to a bowl and add the rest of the breadcrumb ingredients, mixing well. Spread evenly onto a baking tray and bake in the oven for 10–12 minutes, or until golden, mixing halfway.

Wash the kale. If using baby kale, it doesn't need to be steamed. If using regular kale, steam for 10–12 minutes, making sure it is slightly soft but not wilting. Lay the kale on a baking tray lined with paper towels to cool and absorb the excess liquid, patting it dry.

Mix all the dressing ingredients together in a bowl.

Place the kale in a serving bowl. Drizzle with some of the dressing and mix. Add the beetroots, tomatoes and carrots. Drizzle in the rest of the dressing. Sprinkle some breadcrumbs on top. Keep any extra breadcrumbs in the refrigerator in an airtight container and use to add texture to any salad. They will keep for about a week.

Four Herb Salad

This feel-good salad is a fresh, light and healthy addition to any meal. The herbs give it an iron-boosting earthiness which is complemented by the crispy cashews and the sweet and sour dried apricots. The sherry vinegar and date molasses dressing adds a touch of mild acidity. This is my home-comfort salad when I want an energy-boosting bite to eat.

SERVES: 4

30g/1oz/1 cup parsley, washed and chopped without the stalks

30g/1oz/1 cup coriander/cilantro, washed and chopped without the stalks

2 tbsp dill, washed, chopped and stalks removed

15g/½oz/½ cup mint, washed, chopped and stalks removed

2 gem lettuces, washed and finely chopped

60g/2¼oz/½ cup cashews

6–7 dried apricots, diced

For the dressing

4 tbsp extra virgin olive oil

2 tsp sherry vinegar

2 tsp date molasses

Small pinch of salt

Preheat the oven to 180ºC/350ºF/Gas 4.

In a big bowl, mix together the herbs and chopped lettuce. Set aside.

Spread the cashews out on a baking tray and roast in the oven for about 12 minutes until golden. Wait until they've cooled down, then roughly crush with a sharp knife.

Mix the ingredients for the dressing in a small bowl until well combined.

When you are ready to eat, add 2 tablespoons of the dressing to the salad bowl and mix until the leaves are coated. Top with the roasted cashews and dried apricots and add a couple more spoonfuls of the dressing. Mix well and enjoy.

Fine Green Beans & Tomatoes

I love when the simplest methods produce the most delicious dishes, and this is a fine example of that. This recipe was inspired by a Turkish chef I met on holiday years ago, and I have made it many times since. The flavours are unashamedly simple but delicious. It's important to use thin green beans and large beef tomatoes in season, which are full of flavour, alongside good-quality extra virgin olive oil. (I usually do not cook with extra virgin olive oil unless it's on a low heat.)

SERVES: 4

500g/1lb 2oz fine green beans

2 medium onions, finely diced

3 large beef tomatoes, cut into small cubes

5 garlic cloves, thinly sliced

½ tsp salt

1 tsp soft brown sugar

120ml/4fl oz/½ cup extra virgin olive oil

See page 66

Wash the green beans and dry on a clean dish towel/kitchen paper. This is important because you don't want them wet.

In a large, heavy saucepan, place the green beans and spread them out in the pan. Scatter the onions evenly on top, then the tomatoes and the garlic. Sprinkle over the salt and sugar, then drizzle over the olive oil.

Place the pan on a low heat, cover and cook for at least 1–1¼ hours. Your beans will be soft and all the flavours will have merged beautifully together.

Mushroom & Aubergine Quiche

This quiche was a frequent guest in our home, as Amir and the kids love it. It's simple and quick to make, meaning I could whip it up quickly at short notice. If needed, all three cheeses can be swapped for lower-fat options and I promise it will still taste great.

SERVES: 6–8

2 medium onions, diced

3 tbsp rapeseed/canola or
    vegetable oil

300g/10½oz/4 cups mixed
    mushrooms, washed and sliced

1 small aubergine/eggplant,
    washed and cut into small cubes

3 eggs

250g/9oz cottage cheese

250g/9oz light cream cheese

250g/9oz/2 cups grated
    Cheddar cheese

2 tbsp plain/all-purpose flour
    (can be gluten-free)

½ tsp salt

Pinch of coarse ground
    black pepper

See page 67

Preheat the oven to 180°C/350°F/Gas 4.

In a large frying pan, sauté the onions in the oil on a medium heat for 5–6 minutes until golden. Add the mushrooms and aubergine/eggplant, turn the heat up to high and cook for a few minutes until everything is lightly golden. Stir occasionally and make sure the heat is high enough so the mushrooms don't release water. Turn the heat off and let it cool down.

In a large bowl, beat the eggs with a fork. Add the three types of cheese, reserving about four spoonfuls of grated Cheddar to sprinkle on top. Add the vegetables to the bowl and mix well until combined.

Add the flour, salt and pepper and give everything another good mix.

Grease an ovenproof dish 30 x 24cm (12 x 9½in) and pour in the mixture. Sprinkle with the reserved grated Cheddar.

Bake in the oven for 50 minutes until cooked through and the top is golden brown.

White & Red Quinoa with Roasted Sweet Potato, Almonds, Cranberries and a Raw Tahini & Grape Molasses Drizzle

This is my gluten-free, tabbouleh-inspired salad, combining herbs with quinoa instead of bulgur wheat. It has the same satisfying nutty and herby flavours of a traditional tabbouleh. I mix the white and red quinoa together, as the red adds complexity with its crunch and nutty flavour, which is balanced by the fluffier, milder white quinoa. But you can just use one type. This deliciously nutritious dish can be a side or a light vegan meal in its own right.

SERVES: 4

1 small sweet potato (120g/4¼oz), peeled and cut into small cubes

2 tbsp olive oil

Pinch of salt

85g/3oz/½ cup white quinoa

85g/3oz/½ cup red quinoa

40g/1½oz/¼ cup almonds (or roasted almond flakes/slices)

90g/3¼oz rocket, finely chopped

40g/1½oz/½ cup parsley, finely chopped without the stalks

2 tbsp finely chopped coriander/cilantro (stalks removed)

2 tbsp finely chopped mint leaves (stalks removed)

4 spring onions/scallions, finely chopped

2 medium tomatoes, diced

60g/2¼oz/½ cup dried cranberries

4 tbsp pomegranate seeds

A few mint leaves, to garnish

For the dressing

½ tsp salt

Pinch of coarse ground black pepper

½ tsp sumac

2 tbsp lemon juice

3 tbsp extra virgin olive oil

For the tahini and grape molasses drizzle

2 tbsp raw tahini

2 tbsp black grape molasses

Preheat the oven to 200ºC/400ºF/Gas 6.

In a roasting pan, mix the sweet potato cubes with the olive oil and cook in the oven for 30–40 minutes until nicely roasted.

Meanwhile, in a medium-size saucepan, bring 600ml/20fl oz/2½ cups water to the boil on a high heat with a pinch of salt and then add all the quinoa. Reduce the heat, cover and simmer for 20 minutes. Take off the heat and let it stand, covered, for 10 more minutes.

At the same time, spread the almonds out on a baking tray and roast in the oven for 10–12 minutes. Let them cool, then cut lengthways with a sharp knife.

Mix the dressing ingredients in a small bowl until well combined.

Put the rocket and all the herbs into a large bowl. Add the quinoa and mix. Add the spring onions/scallions, chopped tomatoes, cranberries and the dressing and mix until combined.

Spoon the quinoa mixture onto a serving plate. Top with the roasted sweet potato and almonds. Sprinkle the pomegranate seeds on top and drizzle with both the raw tahini and then the black grape molasses. Finally, garnish with mint leaves.

Mum's Mediterranean Vegetable Stew
Ratatouille

My mum used to make an aromatic ratatouille-style stew during my childhood, which had a rich tomato base, onions, red peppers, aubergine/eggplant and sometimes courgettes/zucchini or green beans. She called it *ghivetch*, which means "stew" in some Balkan and Eastern European countries (her mum was born in Odessa), and I loved everything about it. Allowing the vegetables to char before adding the liquid really makes the flavours pop, so don't rush this part as it makes all the difference. Below is my favourite combination of ingredients.

SERVES: 4–6

2–3 tbsp olive oil

1 large onion, diced

3 garlic cloves, sliced

2 red peppers (or yellow/orange), chopped into medium cubes

2 medium tomatoes, chopped

2 aubergines/eggplants, chopped into medium cubes

1 courgette/zucchini, chopped into medium cubes

1 x 400g/14oz can of chopped tomatoes

2 tbsp tomato purée/paste

600ml/20fl oz/2½ cups water

3 thyme sprigs

1 tsp sweet paprika

1 tsp salt

1 tsp soft brown sugar

1 tsp lemon juice

Pinch of coarse ground black pepper

Place a medium-size, heavy pan on a medium heat. Drizzle in a bit of oil and sauté the onion until golden, about 2 minutes. Add the garlic and cook for 1–2 minutes. Push the onion and garlic to the side of the pan and drizzle in a bit more oil. Add the peppers and cook for about 3 minutes, then add the tomatoes and cook for about 5 minutes until softened and slightly charred and they've released a lovely aroma. Add the aubergines/eggplants and courgette/zucchini and mix for a further 4–5 minutes until lightly browned. Mix everything together, including the onions and garlic, for a further minute.

Add the can of tomatoes, mix well and then a minute or so later, add the tomato purée/paste and water, and give it another good stir.

Add the thyme, paprika, salt, sugar, lemon juice and black pepper. Mix everything together and bring to the boil. Reduce the heat and simmer for 1 hour until the vegetables are soft and the flavours have combined.

Peas, Feta & Spinach Salad

Who said you needed lots of ingredients to make a flavoursome dish? Sometimes just three will do! I first tried this at my sister Hillit's home. You not only get tons of flavour from the ingredients and the seasoning, but also very complementary textures. It has since become my daughter's favourite; if there's no spinach, she will just make it with feta cheese and peas in a bowl. Simple and tasty!

SERVES: 2–4

200g/7oz baby spinach, washed and dried

300g/10½oz/2½ cups frozen petit pois

3 tbsp extra virgin olive oil

3 tbsp lemon juice

Pinch of salt

100g/3½oz barrel-aged feta cheese (or any feta cheese)

1 tsp sumac

See page 74

Put the spinach leaves in a large bowl.

Bring a medium-size saucepan of water to the boil over a medium heat and add the peas. Bring back to the boil. Reduce the heat and simmer for 1½–2 minutes, depending on their size. Drain the peas and set aside for 5–10 minutes to steam-dry and cool down.

Add the peas to the spinach. Drizzle with the olive oil and lemon juice and season with the salt. Toss together so the spinach and peas are covered with the oil and lemon dressing. At this point, I suggest letting the salad stand with the dressing. I know it sounds a bit strange, but I prefer to leave it for about 30–40 minutes so the spinach absorbs the flavour from the dressing. The spinach leaves may look a little less pretty, but the flavour is more enhanced.

Crumble the feta cheese by hand and sprinkle on top along with sumac.

Chickpea Salad with Pickled Chillies

This salad is packed with flavour and can be served on its own or alongside any meat or fish dish. It's crunchy and colourful, making it an excellent addition to barbecues, with the pickled chillies giving it a twist that goes very well with the soft chickpeas/garbanzo beans and crunchy vegetables. It's also vegan-friendly.

SERVES: 4

4 red chillies, deseeded and thinly sliced

120ml/4fl oz/½ cup water

120ml/4fl oz/½ cup white wine vinegar (or cider vinegar)

1½ tbsp sugar

1 tsp salt, plus extra for seasoning

½ tsp coriander seeds

175g/6oz/1 cup dried chickpeas/garbanzo beans, soaked in water with 1 tsp of bicarbonate of soda for at least 2 hours (preferably overnight), or 1 x 400g/14oz can of chickpeas, drained and rinsed

20 cherry tomatoes, washed and quartered

1 medium yellow/red pepper, deseeded and chopped into small cubes

½ small red onion, finely chopped

40g/1½oz/1 cup parsley, washed and chopped without the stalks

For the dressing

3 tbsp extra virgin olive oil

2 tbsp lemon juice

1 tsp garlic salt

2 tsp sumac

Pinch of salt

See page 75

Place the chillies in a small heatproof bowl. In a small saucepan, bring to the boil the water, vinegar, sugar, salt and coriander seeds. Remove from the heat, pour over the chillies and let it cool. Leave for at least an hour (longer is even better) for the chillies to pickle and absorb the flavours. (Can be made a day in advance.)

Meanwhile, if you are using dried chickpeas/garbanzo beans, put them into a small saucepan, cover with water to about 5cm (2in) above the chickpeas and place on a medium heat. Sprinkle with a pinch of salt and bring to the boil. Reduce the heat and simmer for about 1 hour until soft. Drain and let them cool down. If using canned chickpeas, you can skip this step.

Place all the vegetables in a medium bowl. Add the chopped parsley and chickpeas to the vegetables and mix well.

Mix the dressing ingredients together in a small bowl until well combined and pour over the salad. Toss until everything is well coated.

Drain the pickled chillies and add them to the salad. Enjoy.

Roasted & Marinated Leeks with Dried Apricots & Manouri Cheese

I love every single ingredient in this salad so much that making it is always a treat. Manouri cheese is a white semi-soft Greek cheese that's a cross between feta cheese and cream cheese; it's not as salty or crumbly as feta. It can be found in big supermarkets, Greek delicatessens or online. The silky leeks taste exquisite with the urfa chilli marinade, which, despite its name, generates a very mild heat with a touch of cacao flavour. Apricots, being sweet and sour, are a fruit I can't resist, as you have probably guessed by the amount they appear in my recipes. Finally, this is all topped with crispy capers and crunchy hazelnuts.

SERVES: 4

18–20 medium leeks

2–3 tbsp extra virgin olive oil

1 tsp urfa chilli flakes, plus extra
  to sprinkle on top

Pinch of salt

1 garlic clove, very finely crushed

3 tbsp rapeseed/canola
  or vegetable oil

4 tbsp capers

80g/2¾oz manouri cheese

30g/1oz/¼ cup hazelnuts,
  roasted and crushed

6–7 dried apricots, thinly sliced

Preheat the oven to 210°C/410°F/Gas 6½.

Wash the leeks well, peel away the top layer, then cut off the green top part and the root end. Cover each leek in foil, arrange them in a roasting pan and roast in the oven for 20–25 minutes.

The leeks should be soft when you prick them with a fork. Remove the foil, peel off the top layer only if stringy (it won't necessarily be, it depends on the type of leek) and cut the flesh into 4–5cm (1½–2in) pieces.

Place the leeks in a glass dish, then add the olive oil, chilli flakes, salt and crushed garlic, and mix. Set aside for 30 minutes.

Meanwhile, in a small saucepan, heat the rapeseed/canola oil on a medium-high heat. Once the oil is hot, add the capers and let them crisp for about 2 minutes. Remove the capers with a slotted spoon and place on a plate with paper towels to absorb the excess oil.

Place the marinated leeks on a serving plate. Crumble the manouri cheese on top. Sprinkle with the roasted hazelnuts, the dried apricots, the crispy capers and some extra urfa chilli flakes.

Basmati Rice with Caramelized Onions, Carrots & Raisins

This is my son Eldar's favourite rice dish. It's the perfect accompaniment for most meat dishes, with a delicious combination of carrots, raisins and onions. It's preferable for the paired meat dish to be without a rich sauce, as the rice has so much flavour of its own. Let the raisins heat up enough to reach the point where they puff up – that's when the flavour changes from being too sweet to just right.

SERVES: 4–6

260g/9½oz/1½ cups white basmati rice

720ml/24fl oz/3 cups water

⅓ tsp ground cumin

⅓ tsp salt

For the caramelized onions

A few tbsp rapeseed/canola or vegetable oil

1 medium onion, sliced into thin strips

2 carrots, grated

4 tbsp raisins

½ tsp salt

⅓ tsp ground turmeric

Pinch of sumac (optional)

Wash the rice until the water runs clear. Place the rice in a medium-size pan, add the water, cumin, salt and 1 tablespoon of oil. Bring to the boil on a medium heat, then reduce to low, cover and simmer for about 15–20 minutes until all the water is absorbed. Put a clean dish towel (or paper towels) around the lid to absorb the steam as it cooks. Leave aside, covered.

Meanwhile, in a large saucepan on a medium-high heat, drizzle 4–5 tablespoons of rapeseed/canola oil. When the oil is heated, add the onion and cook until golden brown and caramelized, about 6–7 minutes. Stir occasionally.

Once the onion has a nice colour, scoop to the side of the pan. Add the carrots and cook for about 2–3 minutes until slightly golden. Make sure you have enough oil, so add some more if needed.

Add the raisins, then stir and cook until they puff up, about 3–4 minutes. Once that's happened, reduce the heat and mix it all together. Add the salt and turmeric and mix well to incorporate.

Add the rice and stir everything together until the rice has turned a golden colour and all the ingredients are evenly mixed. Check the flavour and add a pinch more salt if needed. The rice is ready to eat. You can sprinkle with sumac just before serving, if you like.

Caramelized Butternut Squash with Green Beans & Goat's Cheese

This is a perfect autumn dish but can also be made at any time of the year. Around Halloween, you can even swap out the butternut squash for the sweet Delica or Violina pumpkins that will be in season, meaning you'll have three layers of pumpkin: the pumpkin itself, the seeds and the pumpkin seed oil in the dressing.

SERVES: 4

1 butternut squash, peeled, deseeded and sliced (2–3cm/¾–1¼in thick)

2 tbsp olive oil

Pinch of salt

Pinch of coarse ground black pepper

2 tsp soft brown sugar

200g/7oz green beans

50g/1¾oz/scant ⅓ cup pumpkin seeds

130g/4¾oz soft goat's cheese, torn by hand into small pieces

For the dressing

2 tbsp toasted pumpkin seed oil

2 tbsp vegetable oil

3 tbsp lemon juice

Pinch of salt

Pinch of coarse ground black pepper

2 tsp soft brown sugar

Preheat the oven to 200°C/400°F/Gas 6.

Place the butternut squash in a large bowl, drizzle with the olive oil, then sprinkle with the salt and pepper. Toss until the squash is coated all over.

Line a baking tray with baking parchment and spread out the squash in a single layer. Sprinkle with the brown sugar and roast in the oven for 50 minutes until nicely caramelized.

Meanwhile, put the beans into a small saucepan, cover with water and set on a medium heat. Bring to the boil, reduce the heat and simmer for 5 minutes. Drain and let them steam-dry.

Place the pumpkin seeds in a small frying pan over a medium heat and dry-fry for 5 minutes until golden brown. Stir regularly so they toast evenly. Set aside to cool down.

In a small bowl, make the dressing by mixing all the ingredients together well until the sugar completely dissolves.

Arrange the roasted squash on a large serving plate and scatter the green beans around it. Add the crumbled goat's cheese, drizzle with the dressing and finally sprinkle the pumpkin seeds on top.

Leek, Thyme & Gruyère Galette

A galette is a little pocket of joy; a pastry-based quiche with either a sweet or savoury centre and folded edges that give it an irregular, rustic look. I generally don't like to leave large edges of pastry, but this part is totally up to you.

SERVES: 4–6

25g/1oz butter

1–2 tbsp vegetable oil

400g/14oz leeks, washed and sliced into 5mm/¼in circles

1 tsp soft brown sugar

200g/7oz banana shallots, sliced (about 6)

1 tsp pul biber (Aleppo) chilli flakes, plus a pinch to sprinkle

1 tbsp thick balsamic vinegar (I use Belazu), or 2 tbsp regular balsamic plus ½ tsp sugar, cooked for a few minutes until reduced to a thick syrup consistency

8 thyme sprigs

5 tbsp single cream

¼ tsp salt

1 egg, plus 1 egg to brush on top

100g/3½oz/scant 1 cup grated Gruyère cheese

20g/¾oz grated mozzarella cheese, plus 2 tbsp to sprinkle

1 x 300g/10½oz block of puff pastry

Preheat the oven to 180°C/350°F/Gas 4.

Heat the butter and oil in a large frying pan over a medium-high heat. Add the leeks, sprinkle with the sugar and cook for a few minutes until slightly caramelized and reduced in volume. Add the sliced shallots, reduce the heat to medium and cook, stirring occasionally, for 10 minutes until caramelized. Add the pul biber and balsamic vinegar, stir, cover and cook for another 10 minutes.

Pick the leaves of 4 thyme sprigs (pull the leaves backwards) into a medium-size shallow pan on a low-medium heat, add the cream and let it heat up for a few seconds just so it lightly bubbles but doesn't reach boiling point, then stir and pour into a bowl.

Let it cool for a couple of minutes, before adding the salt and egg and beat. Then add the Gruyère and mozzarella and mix until combined.

Roll out the pastry to whatever shape it creates, probably something between an oval and a square about 26–30cm/10–2in wide. Slide it onto a baking tray lined with baking parchment. Spoon the leek mixture onto the pastry and spread it out evenly, leaving about 2cm/¾in around the edge. Pour the cheese mixture on top and fold the edges of the pastry inwards to create a raised border around the edge.

Sprinkle the extra mozzarella over the top. Snip the remaining 4 thyme sprigs into smaller pieces (about 2.5cm/1in), place them on top and sprinkle with a little extra pul biber.

Beat the second egg in a small bowl and brush over the edges of the pastry. Bake in the oven for 20–25 minutes and watch your beautiful galette turn golden and crisp up.

Pul Biber Chillies

(also called Aleppo chilli flakes)

If you prefer mild over strong heat, as I do, pul biber (Aleppo) chillies are the perfect choice. While their intense orangey-red colour might suggest a powerful kick, they are a mild and delicate chilli. Using pul biber allows me to give a subtle heat to a dish without obscuring its other flavours. They are particularly popular in Turkey but feature across the cuisines of the Eastern Mediterranean and Middle East. When the bright-coloured chilli pods are ripened, they are deseeded and semi-dried, before being crushed coarsely.

Persian Broth with Herbs, Noodles & Dried Lime

This hearty and comforting soup is particularly needed during the winter months. It's full of nostalgic flavours, as it was a go-to comfort dish for me when growing up. It is intensely aromatic and nutrient-rich, with herbs, beans, dried limes and lots more goodness. Don't let the long list of ingredients deter you; it's totally worth it.

SERVES: 6–8

1 large onion, thinly sliced

A few tbsp rapeseed/canola or vegetable oil

Pinch of ground turmeric

¼ tsp dried mint (optional)

90g/3¼oz/½ cup dried chickpeas/garbanzo beans, soaked with 1 tsp of bicarbonate of soda overnight

90g/3¼oz/½ cup dried cannellini beans, soaked in water overnight, or 1 x 400g/14oz can of cannellini beans, drained and rinsed

35–40g/1¼–1½oz/1 cup parsley leaves, washed and chopped

35–40g/1¼–1½oz/1 cup coriander/cilantro leaves, washed and roughly chopped

20g/¾oz/½ cup dill, washed and roughly chopped (no thick stalks)

Leaves from 2 mint sprigs, chopped

100g/3½oz baby spinach, washed

1 tbsp dried fenugreek leaves (optional)

1½ tsp salt

Pinch of coarse ground black pepper

½ tsp ground turmeric

3 dried limes, crushed or pricked with a knife

130g/4¾oz dried Puy lentils, washed

100g/3½oz dried fettuccine

3 tbsp lemon juice

4–5 tbsp thick plain yogurt, to serve

In a large saucepan, sauté the onion in the oil on a medium heat for 3–4 minutes until golden. Add a pinch of turmeric and stir. (Optional: remove a quarter of the onion, place in a small bowl, mix with the dried mint and keep aside for garnish.)

Add the chickpeas/garbanzo beans and cannellini beans to the pan with the onion and mix. Add the herbs, spinach (no need to chop), dried fenugreek, if using, and 1.7–2l/57–68fl oz/7–8 cups of water. Season with the salt, pepper and turmeric. Add the dried limes. Bring to the boil, reduce the heat and simmer covered for 20 minutes.

Add the lentils and cook for about 20 minutes.

Add the fettuccine and cook for a further 10 minutes. If the broth looks too thick, add 1 cup of water and cook for a further 5 minutes.

Drizzle with the lemon juice and taste. Add a touch more salt and black pepper if needed.

When serving, you can put a dollop of thick yogurt and a teaspoon of the onion-mint mixture on top of each portion (if using).

Spelt with Dried Shiitake Mushrooms & Barberries

I always look for wheat alternatives, and the fibre-packed ancient grain spelt is one of my favourite options. I first came across a similar dish on a family holiday in Italy, and my mother-in-law and I enjoyed it so much we complimented the Italian chef that came to chat to us from the kitchen. I've since made spelt in many variations. Here the dried shiitake adds a punch of flavour that goes very well with the nuttiness of the spelt. The tanginess of the barberries cuts through the earthy flavours and the result is super moreish. I hope you like it as much as I do. (I use extra virgin olive oil here as it's important for the flavour, but be careful not to heat the oil too much.)

SERVES: 4

360g/12½oz/2 cups spelt

960ml/34fl oz/4 cups water

30g/1oz/1 cup dried sliced shiitake
  mushrooms

750ml/26fl oz/3¼ cups warm water

5 tbsp extra virgin olive oil,
  plus 2 tbsp to garnish

1 tsp salt

4 tbsp chopped parsley,
  plus extra to garnish

8 thyme sprigs

4 tbsp dried barberries

Wash the spelt well, then place in a medium-size saucepan over a medium-high heat along with the water. Bring to the boil, reduce the heat and simmer for 40 minutes. The water should be completely absorbed and the spelt puffed up.

Meanwhile, place the dried shiitake mushrooms in a small heatproof bowl, pour over the warm water and let them soak for 20 minutes. Drain the mushrooms and place them on paper towels to dry, dabbing with more paper towels on top.

In a large frying pan over a low-medium heat, drizzle 3 tablespoons of extra virgin olive oil. Let the oil warm up, then add the mushrooms, salt, parsley and thyme leaves. (Pick the thyme leaves by pulling them against the direction of growth.) Mix well, then cook for about 5 minutes until the shiitake mushrooms become golden.

Add the barberries and 2 more tablespoons of olive oil, if needed, stir and cook for a further minute.

Add the cooked spelt to the pan and mix until all the ingredients are combined. Cook for another 3–4 minutes, stirring occasionally. Taste to check if you need an extra pinch of salt.

Your dish is ready. Drizzle with extra virgin olive oil and garnish with chopped parsley. Enjoy.

Crispy Cabbage & Onions with Toasted Pine Nuts & Za'atar & Sumac Yogurt

I've always felt that cabbage is an underappreciated vegetable. Aside from being full of nutrients, it absorbs flavours well and is super versatile. In this recipe, it becomes crispy when roasted together with the onions, which makes a delicious contrast to the lemony spiced yogurt.

SERVES: 4

½ red cabbage, thinly sliced

1 large red onion, sliced into thin strips

¼ tsp salt

Pinch of coarse ground black pepper

5 tbsp extra virgin olive oil

2 tbsp pine nuts, toasted

Pinch of sumac

For the yogurt

7 tbsp (200g/7oz/¾ cup) plain yogurt

1 tsp lemon juice

¼ tsp lemon zest

1 tsp za'atar

1 tsp sumac

Preheat the oven to 150°C/300°F/Gas 2.

Put the cabbage and onion in a large bowl. Add the salt, black pepper and olive oil and mix well, massaging the oil into the vegetables.

Line a large baking tray with baking parchment. Spread the cabbage and onion mixture out evenly, then cook in the oven for 1 hour. Mix every 20 minutes. It's important to do this to avoid some parts burning and others not getting crispy enough.

Mix the yogurt with the lemon juice and zest, za'atar and sumac. Spread out the yogurt on a large plate and place the crispy vegetables on top in a nice pile in the middle, then sprinkle with the toasted pine nuts and an extra pinch of sumac.

Pink Couscous with Beetroot, Spicy Chickpeas & Pickled Onions

Couscous is an ideal carrier for a variety of flavours. In this recipe, the couscous becomes pink from the beetroot/beets and absorbs the punchy flavours, creating a vibrant and tasty salad. I've made a couple of suggestions for shortcuts if needed.

SERVES: 4

4 medium beetroots/beets, peeled and cut into small cubes (can buy precooked, but not type in vinegar)

Pinch of salt

Pinch of coarse ground black pepper

2 tbsp light olive oil

200g/7oz/1 cup couscous

240ml/9fl oz/1 cup boiling water

4 tbsp Pickled Red Onions with Sumac (see page 207)

3 spring onions/scallions, finely chopped

4 tbsp lemon juice

3 tbsp extra virgin olive oil

1 tsp pul biber (Aleppo) chilli flakes

¾ tsp salt, for seasoning

1 tbsp roughly chopped mint

For the chickpeas

175g/6oz/1 cup dried chickpeas/ garbanzo beans, soaked overnight or for at least 2 hours with 1 tsp of bicarbonate of soda, or 1 x 400g/14oz can of chickpeas, drained and rinsed

Pinch of salt

2 tbsp extra virgin olive oil

¼ tsp garlic salt or salt

2 tsp pul biber (Aleppo) chilli flakes

Preheat the oven to 200°C/400°F/Gas 6.

If you're using raw beetroots/beets, place them in a baking pan, season with the pinch of salt and black pepper and drizzle with the light olive oil. Cover with foil and cook in the oven for 1½ hours until completely soft. If you're using precooked beetroot, do the same, but only cook for 15-20 minutes. Whether you're cooking them yourself or using precooked beetroots, keep 2 tablespoons of the beetroot juice.

Meanwhile, if you're using soaked dried chickpeas/ garbanzo beans, put them in a saucepan, cover with water to about 5cm (2in) above the chickpeas and place on a medium heat. Add a pinch of salt and bring to the boil. Reduce the heat and simmer for about 1 hour until soft. Drain and let them cool down. Skip this step if you are using canned chickpeas.

In a large, heatproof bowl, place the couscous and pour over the boiling water. Cover and let it stand for 5 minutes, then fluff with a fork. Add the cubed beetroot along with the beetroot juice and mix well until the juice coats the couscous and turns it pink. Add the pickled onions, spring onions/scallions, lemon juice, olive oil, chilli flakes and salt and mix. Transfer to a large serving plate.

Mix the chickpeas with the olive oil, garlic salt and chilli flakes and scatter on top of the pink couscous. Sprinkle with the chopped mint and serve.

Za'atar

Za'atar is a very popular spice in the Middle East. The za'atar plant is a cross between wild thyme and oregano. It is native to Jordan, Lebanon, Syria, Palestine and Israel. After the leaves dry up, they are crushed, then salt, sesame and sumac are added to create the za'atar mix. It has a deep olive colour and an earthy, nutty flavour that's wonderful when dipped with bread, baked in patisserie, sprinkled on top of dips and salads and used as a marinade for meats.

Middle Eastern Lettuce Cups

The lettuce cups at our Shoreditch restaurant, Delamina EAST, have gained a cult following. With their spicy tahini, date molasses, pomegranate seeds and toasted almonds, they pack the flavours of the Middle East into one bite. These vegan lettuce cups can be prepared in advance and assembled just before eating.

Makes: 25

200g/7oz/scant ⅔ cup Tahini (see recipe on page 30)

1½ tbsp pul biber (Aleppo) chilli flakes

250g/9oz dried chickpeas/ garbanzo beans, soaked for at least 2 hours (preferably overnight, with 1 tsp of bicarbonate of soda) or 1 x 400g can of chickpeas, drained and rinsed

Salt and coarse ground black pepper

3 tbsp extra virgin olive oil

1 small aubergine/eggplant, cut into small cubes

250g/9oz green beans

350g/12oz celeriac, grated

3 little gem lettuces, leaves separated, washed and dried

For the dressing

2 tbsp lemon juice

3 tbsp extra virgin olive oil

1 small garlic clove, finely crushed

To serve

Flaked/sliced almonds, toasted

4 tbsp pomegranate seeds

2 spring onions/scallions, finely chopped

4 tbsp date molasses

Preheat the oven to 190°C/375°F/Gas 5.

Mix the tahini and pul biber in a small bowl. Set aside.

If using dried chickpeas/garbanzo beans, put them into a small saucepan, cover with water to about 5cm (2in) above the chickpeas and place on a medium heat. Sprinkle with a pinch of salt and bring to the boil. Reduce the heat and simmer for about 1 hour until soft. Drain and transfer to a bowl to cool. If using canned chickpeas, you can skip this step. Add 1 tablespoon of olive oil and some salt and pepper and mix.

Meanwhile, place the aubergine/eggplant in a small bowl, drizzle with the remaining olive oil and season with salt and pepper. Place baking parchment on a baking tray and spread out the aubergine in a single layer. Cook in the oven for about 25–30 minutes until golden brown and soft, mixing halfway.

Put the beans into a small saucepan, cover with water and set on a medium heat. Bring to the boil, reduce the heat and simmer for 5 minutes. Drain, leave to cool slightly, then cut into 1cm/½in pieces.

Put the celeriac in a medium bowl. Make the dressing by mixing the lemon juice, olive oil and garlic in a small bowl. Pour the dressing over the celeriac and mix well until the celeriac is covered. Add the beans, chickpeas and aubergine and mix.

Whisk the tahini with a fork to bring the flavours together and you'll see it is now pinkish in colour. Drizzle on top of the vegetables. Mix well.

Take a lettuce leaf and place a heaped spoonful of the mix in the middle. Sprinkle with some almonds, pomegranate seeds and spring onions/scallions and drizzle with date molasses. Repeat with the rest.

Roasted & Glazed Apricots with Asparagus, Topped with Sunflower & Sesame Seed Clusters

This fresh salad tastes like the beginning of summer. The apricots give such a delicate taste, not too sweet, not too sour, which feels fitting when the weather starts to improve. I usually make this salad in spring when both apricots and asparagus are in season.

SERVES: 4

1 bunch of asparagus (about 16 small asparagus spears)

2 tbsp extra virgin olive oil, plus extra for griddling

Pinch of salt

Pinch of coarse ground black pepper

8 apricots, washed, cut in half and pitted

2–3 tbsp date molasses

4 thyme sprigs

60g/2¼oz lamb's lettuce, washed and dried

60g/2¼oz rocket, washed and dried

For the sunflower and sesame seed clusters

2 tbsp sunflower seeds

2 tbsp sesame seeds

1 tsp nigella seeds

1½ tbsp maple syrup

For the dressing

1 tbsp balsamic vinegar

1 tbsp red wine vinegar

1 tbsp soy sauce

2 tbsp extra virgin olive oil

2 tbsp vegetable oil

1 tsp thick balsamic reduction (I prefer Belazu) or date molasses

Preheat the oven to 200ºC/400ºF/Gas 6.

Blanch the asparagus in boiling water for 5 minutes. Drain and dab with paper towels to dry. Place in a large square dish, drizzle with the 2 tablespoons of oil, sprinkle with the salt and pepper and mix well until coated.

In a large shallow pan on a medium heat – I like to use a griddle/grill pan to get the griddle marks – drizzle a little oil. When hot, cook the asparagus for about 2–3 minutes on each side.

Lay the apricots, cut side up, on a baking tray lined with baking parchment. Brush with the date molasses and sprinkle with the thyme leaves (pull the leaves backwards). Roast in the oven for about 20–30 minutes or more (depending on the size) until caramelized and softened. Leave aside to cool.

Meanwhile, to make the clusters, place a medium pan on a medium heat and dry-fry the sunflower seeds for 2–3 minutes, stirring them constantly so they toast evenly. Add the sesame seeds and stir for about 2 minutes. Keep an eye on them as they can burn very quickly. When they start to colour, add the nigella seeds and give it another minute, then add the maple syrup. Mix well to coat everything for about 2 minutes, then tip onto a baking tray to cool. When at room temperature, break up to create clusters.

Mix the ingredients of the dressing until well combined. Place the mixed leaves on a large serving plate, drizzle over half the dressing and toss until coated. Arrange the asparagus nicely on top and place the roasted apricots in between them. Sprinkle with the seed clusters and drizzle over the rest of the dressing.

Chopped Garden Salad with Olives

This salad is inspired by my Aunt Dorit. Everything she makes is so tasty; going for dinner there means you know you're in for a treat. Even the simplest dishes are transformed under her spell. We've always exchanged recipes, but years of living in different countries has meant we haven't been able to enjoy each other's dishes as much as we'd like. It was at hers that I first tried green olives added to a classic chopped salad, a simple touch that really elevated the flavours. The crunchy garden vegetables and nigella seeds make it a celebration of colours and textures, an ideal fresh salad to complement any meal. I like to use nocellara olives as they are large, easy to handle and have a delicate flavour that is not overpowering.

SERVES: 4

2 spring onions/scallions, finely sliced

3 tbsp lemon juice

2 medium tomatoes

2 small cucumbers or ½ large cucumber

1 yellow or red pepper, deseeded

5–6 radishes

10 pitted nocellara olives

½ tsp salt

3 tbsp extra virgin olive oil

1 tsp sumac, plus a little extra to sprinkle on top

1 tsp nigella seeds

Leaves from 2 mint sprigs, roughly chopped

See page 102

Place the spring onions/scallions in a small bowl with 1 tablespoon of the lemon juice. This will take the edge off and will prevent the aftertaste that some people are sensitive to.

Chop the rest of the vegetables into very small cubes.

Slice the nocellara olives into thin slivers.

Place all the vegetables in a large bowl, including the spring onions with the lemon juice, along with the olives. Give it a mix, then add the 2 remaining tablespoons of lemon juice, salt, olive oil, sumac and nigella seeds and mix again well.

Transfer to a serving dish and sprinkle with the mint and extra sumac.

Summer Salad

My mother was always very sensitive to fresh onions, so I developed a method that takes the edge off. Place the chopped onions in a little bowl with vinegar or lemon juice and let it sit while you prepare the rest of the salad. The acidity will interact with the onions, reduce the intensity of their flavour and lightly pickle them. I love every shape and form of tomatoes, so choose whichever ones you want and top with za'atar croutons to create a beautifully vibrant salad.

SERVES: 4

½ small red onion, finely chopped

3–4 slices of sourdough bread

2 tbsp extra virgin olive oil

1 tbsp za'atar

2 tbsp pine nuts

300g/10½oz/2 cups cherry tomatoes, halved

1 yellow pepper, deseeded and chopped into medium cubes

50g/1¾oz/½ cup pitted kalamata olives, halved

For the dressing

1 tbsp sherry vinegar

3½ tbsp extra virgin olive oil

2 tsp za'atar

½ small garlic clove, crushed and mashed into a smooth paste (see page 30)

See page 103

Preheat the oven to 180°C/350°F/Gas 4 and line an ovenproof dish with baking parchment.

Place the chopped onion in a small bowl, add the sherry vinegar (for the dressing) and set aside.

Tear the slices of bread into a bowl. Drizzle with the olive oil and sprinkle with the za'atar, then toss until evenly coated. Spread out in the lined ovenproof dish and cook in the oven for 15–20 minutes. Set aside to cool down.

Meanwhile, dry-fry the pine nuts in a small shallow pan on a low-medium heat. Toss and stir for a few minutes, keeping an eye on them so they don't burn. When golden brown, set aside to cool.

Arrange the tomatoes, yellow pepper and olives on a serving plate. Scatter the crispy croutons on top.

Add the rest of the dressing ingredients to the small bowl with the onion. Mix well and drizzle over the salad. Toss well until everything is coated, then sprinkle with the toasted pine nuts and serve.

Courgette, Carrot & Feta Fritters

Fritters remind me of Hanukkah, a festival that is usually celebrated around the same time as Christmas. Traditionally, people will light candles for eight days and eat donuts as well as latkes, which are basically potato fritters. I always preferred the savoury fritters to the sweet donuts, especially my mum's fritters, as she added sweet potatoes to the mix, giving them a unique, delicate flavour. Inspired by her recipe, I find that these courgette/zucchini, carrot and feta fritters are always a crowd-pleaser and feel even more special when paired with the yogurt and mint dip. One tip when cooking: be careful not to burn the outside of the fritters before they are fully cooked inside. This means making sure the oil is hot enough so that they sizzle when placed in the pan, but not so hot that they reach smoking point (at this point, you shouldn't use the oil any more). I find rapeseed/canola oil works best.

SERVES: 4–6

2 courgettes/zucchini, peeled and coarsely grated

2 carrots, peeled and coarsely grated

1 tsp salt

2 eggs

Zest of ½ lemon (optional)

3 tbsp gluten-free plain/all-purpose flour (or any flour of your choice)

100g/3½oz feta cheese, crumbled

50ml/2fl oz/¼ cup rapeseed/canola oil or any vegetable oil you prefer

For the dip

100g/3½oz/generous ½ cup plain yogurt

Leaves from 2 mint sprigs, washed and finely chopped

Place the grated vegetables in a sieve/fine-mesh strainer over a large bowl and mix with the salt. Leave for 10–15 minutes. Squeeze out and discard the excess liquid.

In a large bowl, mix the grated vegetables with the eggs and lemon zest, if using. Add the flour and feta cheese and mix well.

Put a large frying pan on a medium heat, pour in about a third of the oil and heat. Carefully add a tablespoon of the vegetable batter, sliding it into the hot oil; it should sizzle when it hits the oil. Flatten it out slightly. Add a few more to fill the pan. When each becomes golden brown underneath, flip it over.

Prepare a large plate with paper towels next to the pan. When both sides of the fritters are lovely and golden, take them out and place on the lined plate to allow the excess oil to be absorbed. Continue in the same way, adding oil to the pan and working your way through the batter.

To make the dip, spoon the yogurt into a bowl. Add the mint and mix well.

Hero Dishes & Sharing Plates

Being the child of parents of mixed heritage

has exposed me to many flavours and culinary traditions. A simple example of how this comes to life is the Hearty Chicken & Herb Soup (see page 130) my parents would make on Friday nights. At my grandmother's home in the kibbutz, we would have the traditionally Eastern European clear chicken soup, but at our home it took on a new shape, with my father adding chickpeas, plenty of herbs – parsley, coriander and dill – as well as spices like turmeric and cumin. The soup evolved with creativity and love through the lens of different cultures, everyone enjoying each other's versions but adding their own influences to the literal and metaphorical soup.

As far as mealtimes go, Friday night has a special place in my heart. It's not just the food that is particularly tasty and more invested in than usual, but the fact that you are gathered with your nearest and dearest, sharing stories and discussing the world, all in the comfort of someone's home. I didn't have a religious upbringing but the tradition of having a big family meal on Friday night is something I cherished and connected to. Food, company and love are an important triangle for me. When we were growing up, we always ate together as a family. My dad was a high school teacher and entrepreneur and was always on the move, full of energy. But whenever he would eat at home, irrespective of the time, he would call us to join him, so that he always had company. He would never just snack and pop back out; eating was a communal ritual. A big part of how my father expressed his love for us was through food. He enjoyed feeding us; it was important for him that we ate together and enjoyed it (which was easy, as it was always delicious). I saw this play out later with my children, his grandchildren: when we went to visit, he was ready to spoil them with delicious food and revel in their satisfaction. As soon as their plates were cleared, he was always ready to hand out seconds! So, I suppose that for me and my family, food was synonymous with care, love, generosity and being together. I hope these recipes can help create similar memories for you.

The recipes here include a selection of showstoppers, regular go-tos and comforting dishes. They all show my love for an abundance of flavour and good nutrition, and were created for a home cook, with an acute awareness of everyday practicalities such as time limitations and sourcing of certain ingredients.

Salmon Carpaccio with Crunchy Radishes, Chives & Nigella Seeds

I usually make this carpaccio as a first course, but it can also work as a fresh and light main, accompanied by a small salad. It's easier to make than it sounds yet looks and tastes fabulous. It's important to buy sushi-grade salmon and put it in the freezer, so that you can prepare it when it's semi-frozen, which makes it easier to slice and gives the final presentation a very professional look. Each layer of ingredients contributes to the harmony of flavours and textures, so try not to skip any! You have the soft, succulent salmon, topped with the juicy acidic tomato flesh, along with the crunchiness of the radishes and earthiness of the nigella seeds. And, of course, sumac – my favourite spice.

SERVES: 4

200g/7oz sushi-grade salmon (skinless)

1 medium-size plum tomato

1 tsp pink Himalayan salt

Salt and freshly ground black pepper, to season

2 radishes, washed and sliced into thin discs

4 chives, cut into 1cm/½in pieces

1 tbsp nigella seeds

3 tbsp lemon juice

3 tbsp extra virgin olive oil

2 tbsp lime juice

1 tsp date molasses

1 tsp sumac

Two or three hours before you want to start this recipe, put the salmon in the freezer. This will allow you to easily slice it. When you are ready to start making the recipe, take it out of the freezer and slice it very thinly. Arrange nicely on a serving plate.

Slice off the tip of the tomato, hold it against a grater and start grating until you are left just with the skin. Be very careful as you get closer to the grater. Better to leave more tomato flesh than hurt your fingers!

Sprinkle the salt evenly on the fish. Season the tomato flesh with salt and pepper and spoon over the fish. Scatter over the radishes, chives and nigella seeds. Drizzle with the lemon juice and olive oil.

Mix the lime juice and date molasses and drizzle over the salmon. Sprinkle with sumac before serving.

Seared Tuna with Sesame & Barberries

This lovely light tuna dish can either be a delicious main or a delicate start to the meal. It's important that the tuna is just seared so it stays pink in the middle and can absorb the flavours from the dressing. I prefer to use a griddle/grill pan, but any frying pan will do. It's a great dish to share and you can easily play with the quantities depending on whether you serve it as a first course or a main. The barberries add a touch of zest and colour. Baharat is a fragrant and popular spice mix in the region used in stews, rice, vegetable dishes, and as a marinade for meats and fish. Both ingredients can be found in most Middle Eastern shops.

SERVES: 4

4 tuna fillets (sashimi grade)

4 tbsp sesame seeds

Pinch of salt

1 tbsp rapeseed/canola
  or vegetable oil

3 tbsp dried barberries

For the tuna rub

1 tsp baharat

½ tsp salt

Pinch of coarse ground
  black pepper

4 tbsp olive oil

For the dressing

5 tbsp extra virgin olive oil

½ tsp baharat

2½ tbsp lemon juice

3 tsp honey

¼ tsp salt

Pinch of coarse ground
  black pepper

For the rub, mix the baharat, salt and pepper together with the olive oil and rub it over the tuna on both sides. Set aside.

In a bowl, whisk together all the ingredients for the dressing until combined. Set aside.

Toast the sesame seeds in a dry frying pan on a medium heat, stirring constantly. Keep an eye on them and don't be tempted to increase the heat, as they can burn very quickly, making the sesame bitter. It should take about 3–4 minutes until they are golden and release a lovely aroma. Set aside to cool down.

Brush a griddle/grill pan with the rapeseed/canola oil and place on a high heat. When the pan is hot, sear the tuna fillets for 30–40 seconds on each side. The tuna should be sealed with griddle marks on both sides but remain pink in the middle. Remove from the pan and slice into 1cm/½in pieces.

Arrange the tuna slices on a serving dish, drizzle with the dressing, sprinkle with the toasted sesame seeds and top with the barberries.

Salmon Ras-el-Hanout & Pomegranate Molasses with Sweet Potato Purée

I use pomegranate molasses often in my kitchen. It is deliciously tart, and in this recipe the sharpness of their flavour cuts through the rich salmon so well. With the addition of ras-el-hanout, you are immediately transported to the Middle East. Ras-el-hanout translated from Arabic is "head of the shop". It's a popular spice mix throughout the Middle East and is a blend of the premium spices the shop has to offer, as the name suggests.

SERVES: 4

4 salmon fillets

4 small sweet potatoes (about 500g/1lb 2oz in total), peeled and cut into medium cubes

4 medium potatoes (about 400g/14oz in total) peeled and cut into medium cubes

Pinch of salt

1 tbsp rapeseed/canola or vegetable oil

4 tbsp olive oil

1 tbsp lemon juice

1 tsp sumac

1 tsp salt

For the marinade

4 tbsp pomegranate molasses

1 tsp ras el hanout

2 tsp date molasses

1 tsp garlic salt

To serve

A few dill sprigs

4 tbsp pomegranate seeds

Preheat the oven to 180°C/350°F/Gas 4.

First make the marinade by mixing all the ingredients together until well combined and the garlic salt has dissolved. Place the salmon in a dish, then pour the marinade over the salmon and leave in the refrigerator for 1–2 hours. If you can leave it longer it will soak up the flavours even more.

In a medium-size saucepan, cook all the potatoes in boiling water with a pinch of salt for about 30 minutes depending on the size, or until they are very soft.

Meanwhile, place a frying pan on a medium heat and drizzle in the rapeseed/canola oil. When hot, gently add the fish, skin-side down, and cook for 30 seconds, then turn over and cook for another 30 seconds. (Keep the dish with the marinade.) Transfer to an ovenproof dish and pour over the remaining marinade. Cook in the oven for 8–10 minutes.

In a small bowl, whisk the olive oil, lemon juice, sumac and salt to combine.

Drain the potatoes, transfer to a bowl and mash to a medium-smooth consistency. Add the olive oil and lemon mixture and mash again until smooth.

Spoon the sweet potato purée onto a large serving plate, place the salmon on top and sprinkle with the dill and pomegranate seeds.

Halibut in Red Pepper Sauce with Chickpeas & Kalamata Olives

This thick, rich, red pepper sauce is full of flavour and works very well with halibut, although if you can't source halibut, salmon works just as well. This dish has a nice kick to it, so if you're not a fan of spicy food, reduce the chilli to just a small pinch, or replace with pul biber (Aleppo) chilli flakes, which are very mild. Scoop up the sauce with bread or fluffy pitta!

SERVES: 4

4 halibut fillets

2 tsp sweet paprika

1½ tsp salt

6 tbsp rapeseed/canola or vegetable oil

2 red peppers, deseeded and cut into strips

Handful of parsley, washed and stalks removed

Handful of coriander/cilantro, washed and stalks removed

8–10 garlic cloves, cut into thick slices

2 small fresh red chillies, sliced, or 1 tsp pul biber (Aleppo) chilli flakes

Pinch of coarse ground black pepper

85g/3oz/½ cup dried chickpeas/garbanzo beans, soaked in water with 1 tsp of bicarbonate of soda overnight, or ½ x 400g/14oz can of chickpeas, drained and rinsed

50g/1¾oz/½ cup pitted kalamata olives, cut in half

240ml/9fl oz/1 cup water

Season the fish with 1 teaspoon of paprika and 1 teaspoon of salt and set aside.

Place a shallow, heavy saucepan on a medium-high heat and drizzle in half the oil. Add the peppers, herbs, garlic and red chillies (or chilli flakes). Sprinkle with the remaining 1 teaspoon of paprika and ½ teaspoon of salt and a pinch of black pepper and drizzle with the rest of the oil. Cook for 5 minutes.

Add the chickpeas/garbanzo beans and olives, reduce the heat and cook for 15 minutes.

Place the fish in the sauce. Slowly pour in the water at the side of the pan (don't pour it over the whole dish) so that the fish is almost covered. Add a bit more if needed. Increase the heat and bring to the boil, then reduce the heat and simmer for about 30 minutes. Half-cover the pan so the sauce reduces but not too much. From time to time, spoon some of the sauce over the fish to keep it moist. The sauce should end up lovely and thick but not too dry. Check the seasoning and add a touch more salt if needed before serving.

Cod Chermoula, Israeli Couscous with Artichokes & Dill Yogurt

I'm particularly proud of this dish. During my childhood, we used to eat plenty of fish, but cod was my least favourite. I had to find a way to make it exciting, so that it would be just as delicious to me. This recipe includes Israeli couscous (*ptitim*), which is a popular dish that children in Israel grow up eating. Once you add artichokes to the al dente couscous, paired with the rich chermoula sauce and creamy dill yogurt, you've got an explosion of taste and textures. I make this repeatedly; it is very popular both at home and at Delamina.

SERVES: 6

6 cod fillets

For the chermoula sauce

2 tsp sweet paprika

2 tsp pul biber (Aleppo) chilli flakes

2 tsp ground cumin

1 tsp salt

2 garlic cloves, crushed

1 tbsp finely chopped parsley

1 tbsp finely chopped coriander/
  cilantro

Juice of 2 small lemons

3½ tbsp extra virgin olive oil

For the Israeli couscous

2 tbsp any type of vegetable oil

250g/9oz/scant 1½ cups Israeli
  couscous

300ml/10½fl oz/1¼ cups water

1 tsp salt

4 tsp garlic oil

2 tsp pul biber (Aleppo) chilli flakes

100g/3½oz marinated artichokes
  (good quality, from a jar), drained
  and sliced into 2cm/¾in pieces

For the dill yogurt sauce

300g/10½oz/scant 1¼ cups
  plain yogurt

Handful of dill, washed and
  finely chopped

Pinch of salt

Mix together all the dry chermoula ingredients, including the garlic and herbs, then add the lemon juice, mixing well until combined. Add the olive oil slowly and continue mixing until combined.

Wash and pat dry the cod fillets. Place them in an ovenproof dish with a few spoonfuls of the chermoula sauce and marinate in the refrigerator for about 30 minutes (longer if you have time). Keep the rest of the sauce aside; you will need it later.

Preheat the oven to 180°C/350°F/Gas 4. Place the cod in the oven and cook for about 20–25 minutes.

Meanwhile, make the couscous. Place a medium saucepan on a medium heat with the oil. Add the couscous and toast until golden brown. It is important not to step away from the pan during this process and to mix continuously. Make sure it doesn't get too dark, as it doesn't taste pleasant. Once the couscous is golden, pour in the water and add ½ teaspoon of the salt. Bring to boil, reduce the heat, cover and simmer for 10 minutes. Remove from the heat and let it stand, covered, for about 5 minutes. Remove the lid and fluff the couscous with a fork.

Add the garlic oil, chilli flakes, remaining salt and the artichokes to the couscous and mix well. Taste and adjust the seasoning if necessary.

To make the dill yogurt sauce, mix the yogurt, dill and a pinch of salt until well combined. To serve, spread the yogurt sauce on each plate, then spoon the couscous on top, add the fish and drizzle the chermoula generously over everything.

Brill with White Wine, Parsley & Sumac Sauce

I like using brill for this recipe, as it has a delicate and almost sweet flavour that works very well with the white wine and sumac sauce. If you can't find brill, try to replace it with turbot, but otherwise any white fish that has a slightly more delicate flavour and texture will do, like Dover sole, lemon sole, seabass or sea bream.

SERVES: 4

4 brill fillets

Pinch each of salt, freshly ground black pepper and sumac

2 tbsp extra virgin olive oil

2 tbsp rapeseed/canola or vegetable oil

For the sauce

2 tbsp butter

1 shallot or ½ small red onion, finely chopped

2 garlic cloves, finely chopped

2 tbsp finely chopped parsley (tough stalks removed), plus extra to serve

1½ tbsp plain/all-purpose flour (can be gluten-free)

360ml/12fl oz/1⅓ cups cold milk (I use oat milk)

6 tbsp dry white wine

⅓ tsp salt

Pinch of coarse ground black pepper

1 tsp sumac, plus an extra pinch to serve

Season the fish with a pinch each of salt, pepper and sumac. Drizzle with the olive oil and set aside.

Melt the butter in a heavy saucepan on a medium-low heat. Once heated, add the shallot or onion and sauté for 2–3 minutes until translucent. Add the garlic and parsley and cook for another 3 minutes.

Turn the heat down to low. Add the flour, mix it in well for a minute, then add the cold milk while constantly stirring. Start with a third of the milk and mix vigorously, and when the lumps disappear, add another third and keep stirring, and finally add the rest of the milk. Add the white wine and keep stirring constantly. If it looks too thick, you can add more milk. It should be smooth with a creamy consistency.

Add the salt, pepper and sumac. Keep on a very low heat, stirring occasionally, while you cook the fish.

Heat the rapeseed/canola oil in a large frying pan on a medium-high heat. When the oil is hot, gently add the fish and cook for a few minutes on each side, depending on the thickness of the fish. It should be cooked through but not dry.

Transfer the fish to serving plates. Drizzle the sauce on the fish and sprinkle with extra sumac and chopped parsley.

Whole Seabass with Herbs, Lime & Orange Zest

Fish lovers are often divided between off or on the bone. I'm certainly the latter and won't let anyone clean the fish for me at any restaurant – I enjoy doing it myself, and our kids are the same! I inherited my love of fish from my dad who liked them in any shape or form, including cured fish, herring and the very Eastern European gefilte fish, which are poached fishcakes traditionally eaten during the Passover festival. If you prefer to eat a whole fish but don't like to deal with the bones, at our Delaminas, we serve it "canoed", meaning the fish is deboned but kept whole with only a slit in the side.

SERVES: 2–4

2 whole seabass (about 400g/
  14oz each)

4 slices of lime (sliced into circles)

Chopped parsley, to garnish

For the marinade

4 garlic cloves, crushed

5 tbsp roughly chopped parsley

4 tbsp olive oil

2 tsp orange zest

2 tsp lime zest

1 tbsp lemon juice

½ tsp sumac

1 tsp salt

½ tsp sweet paprika

For the dressing

2 tbsp lemon juice

1 tsp orange juice

½ tsp sumac

Pinch of salt

2 tbsp olive oil

2 tbsp garlic-infused oil
  (or ¼ tsp pureed garlic ,
  see page 30)

Preheat the oven to 200°C/400°F/Gas 6 and line a baking tray with baking parchment.

Clean the fish and pat dry with paper towels. With a sharp knife, make three slits diagonally on each side of the fish.

In a small bowl, mix all the ingredients for the marinade. Rub the fish with a generous amount of the marinade, including inside, making sure you push it into the slits that you made.

Place the lime slices inside the fish, 2 slices each. Transfer the fish to the lined baking tray and cook in the oven for about 25 minutes (depending on the size of the fish). The fish should be cooked through but not too dry.

Meanwhile, mix together the ingredients for the dressing except the oils, then slowly add the oils while constantly whisking.

Place the fish on a serving plate and drizzle with the dressing, then garnish with some chopped parsley.

Crispy Sea Bream Fillet with Charred Cherry Tomatoes & Tahini Yogurt

As I'm sensitive to gluten, I always look for creative ways to replace flour. This recipe uses roasted rice for the coating that makes it very crispy and fun to eat, so it's a good one to save for those family meals! It's important to sieve the ground toasted rice through a sieve/fine-mesh strainer to make sure no big pieces are left.

SERVES: 4

90g/3¼oz/½ cup rice

2 tbsp finely chopped parsley

1 tsp chopped rosemary

1 tsp salt

½ tsp sweet paprika

4 sea bream fillets

3 tbsp rapeseed/canola
  or vegetable oil

For the cherry tomatoes

400g/14oz cherry tomatoes

2 tbsp light olive oil

Pinch of salt

Pinch of coarse ground
  black pepper

4 garlic cloves, sliced

Handful of parsley, washed
  and roughly chopped

10 thyme sprigs, leaves picked

For the tahini yogurt

4 tbsp plain yogurt or labneh

3 tbsp Tahini dip (see page 30)

1 tsp pul biber (Aleppo) chilli flakes

1 tbsp lemon juice

Pinch of salt

See page 126

Preheat the oven to 240ºC/475ºF/Gas 9.

In a medium bowl, toss the tomatoes together with the olive oil, salt and pepper until they're coated with the oil. Transfer to an ovenproof dish and roast in the oven for 20 minutes until they start to char and blister. Remove the dish from the oven, sprinkle the tomatoes with the garlic, parsley and thyme leaves, and return to the oven for 15 more minutes.

Meanwhile, place a frying pan on a medium heat and toast the rice for about 3 minutes, stirring occasionally so it toasts evenly. It's ready when it has turned slightly golden and releases a lovely aroma.

Let the rice cool for a few minutes before transferring to a food processor. Blitz to a fine powder, then pass through a sieve/fine-mesh strainer (this is important in order to avoid large, hard pieces). Add the parsley, rosemary, salt and paprika and mix. Spread the mixture out on baking parchment.

Wash the fish but don't dry it. Dip each fillet into the rice mixture on both sides, and press so it's evenly covered.

Heat the rapeseed/canola oil in a shallow pan on a medium heat. When the oil is hot, gently add the sea bream fillets, skin-side down, and cook for about 2 minutes. When golden, turn and cook the other side for another 2 minutes.

Make the tahini yogurt by mixing all the ingredients together. You can serve it on the side for dipping, or spread a generous dollop on each plate, place the fish on top and scatter with the charred tomatoes.

Za'atar Prawns with Roasted Peppers, Paprika Aioli & Caperberries

Za'atar, a very popular spice mix throughout the Middle East, is such a versatile spice, often added to bread or sprinkled on dips and salads. I love cooking with it, especially chicken and prawns/shrimp, as it adds a salty nuttiness. This prawn dish with roasted red peppers and paprika aioli is an all-time favourite at Delamina.

SERVES: 4

28–30 medium-size raw peeled prawns/shrimp, washed

2 red peppers, deseeded and sliced into 2cm/¾in strips

2 tbsp olive oil

Pinch of salt

Pinch of coarse ground black pepper

2 tbsp lemon juice

16 caperberries

For the marinade

6 tsp za'atar

4 garlic cloves, crushed

Zest of 2 lemons

6–7 tbsp light olive oil

For the paprika aioli

1 egg yolk

1 garlic clove, crushed and mashed to a smooth paste (see page 30)

2 tbsp lemon juice

2 tbsp water

¼ tsp salt

1½ tsp paprika

4½ tbsp vegetable oil

See page 127

Preheat the oven to 200°C/400°F/Gas 6.

In a bowl, mix together all the ingredients for the marinade until well combined. Add the prawns/shrimp and toss until they are all coated, then place in the refrigerator to marinate for at least 30 minutes.

Mix the pepper slices with 1 tablespoon of olive oil, the salt and pepper and spread out on a baking parchment-lined baking tray. Roast in the oven for 30 minutes until they look soft and charred.

Meanwhile, put all the ingredients for the paprika aioli into a food processor and blitz until smooth. The quantities here are for a mini food processor. If yours is a large size, you will need to double the amount, as this quantity will be too small for it to work.

When you're ready to cook, take the prawns out of the marinade and drizzle with the lemon juice.

Heat the remaining 1 tablespoon of oil in a large frying pan on a medium-high heat. Once hot, add the prawns and cook for 1½–2 minutes on each side until they change colour and are slightly charred with some crispy za'atar bits on them.

Arrange the prawns on a serving plate, scraping the za'atar mix from the pan on top, as it is full of flavour. Place the roasted peppers in between the prawns. Add dollops of the aioli around the plate to dip the prawns in, scatter over the caperberries and enjoy.

Hearty Chicken & Herb Soup
The Jewish Penicillin

I love making this chicken soup, its fragrant smell filling the house with a nostalgic aroma. It's a traditional festive dish eaten by Jewish families during Friday night dinners, yet has made its way onto many people's tables – a truly heart-warming dish sometimes referred to as "Jewish penicillin" because of its nourishing effect. Each family has its own variation, with recipes often passed down through generations, and mine combines elements from my parents' mixed heritage. I make several variations, depending on what's in the refrigerator, but always with onions, carrots, celery and herbs – the rest is optional! Sweet potatoes are delicious, as are leeks and courgettes/zucchini. Don't be scared to add a generous helping of herbs; they wilt and can be removed before serving, but give a special flavour and aroma you don't want to miss. A handful of chickpeas/garbanzo beans, brown rice or pearl barley make it more brothy, so be adventurous!

SERVES: 6–8

6 chicken pieces (thighs, drumsticks and any bones for added flavour) or 1 small whole chicken

2 onions, chopped into medium-size wedges

3 carrots, chopped into thick discs

2 celery stalks, chopped

1 sweet potato, chopped into medium-size chunks

90g/3¼oz/½ cup dried chickpeas/garbanzo beans, soaked in water and 1 tsp of bicarbonate of soda overnight or 200g/7oz canned chickpeas, drained and rinsed, or brown rice or pearl barley if you prefer (optional)

Bunch of parsley

Bunch of coriander/cilantro

Bunch of dill

2 tsp ground turmeric

1½ tsp ground cumin

2 tsp salt

Pinch of freshly ground black pepper

Wash the chicken and place in a large saucepan, adding enough water to cover the chicken, about 2l/68fl oz/8½ cups. Bring to the boil and skim off and discard the foam from the top of the water.

Add all the chopped vegetables to the pan. Add the chickpeas/garbanzo beans (or rice or pearl barley), if using.

Wash the herbs well and tie them together with string or a rubber band and add to the pan. Add the spices and seasoning. Bring to the boil, then reduce the heat, cover and simmer for 1½ hours until the chicken is cooked.

To serve, shred the chicken, removing the bones, and return it to the broth.

As children, we loved our chicken soup with tiny yellow croutons. They can be found in supermarkets in the kosher aisle.

Roasted Turkey Drumsticks with Garlic, Caramelized Sweet Potatoes & Onions

My mother introduced me to the wonderful world of cooking turkey, a lean and healthy protein. She made this dish for us many times and it was always succulent and delicious, contrary to the perception many people have of this meat! I only realized later that for most families in the UK, turkey is only cooked at Christmas and often roasted for hours as one whole bird; eating turkey as often as we did wasn't common. This dish is full of flavour and is a Sunday classic in our home.

SERVES: 4

2 turkey drumsticks (around
  800g/1lb 12oz each), skin-on

2 garlic cloves, sliced lengthways

2 tsp sweet paprika

2 tsp garlic salt

5 tbsp olive oil, plus 2 tbsp for
  the vegetables

4 sweet potatoes, peeled and
  cut into medium chunks

8 small onions, cut in half

Preheat the oven to 200°C/400°F/Gas 6.

Wash the drumsticks and dry them well with paper towels. (It's important that they are completely dry.) With a sharp, pointed knife, pierce the turkey legs a few times and insert the slices of garlic.

In a small bowl, mix the paprika and garlic salt with the oil. Generously brush the drumsticks with the paprika oil all over.

Place the drumsticks in a large, ovenproof dish. Scatter the sweet potatoes and onions around them and brush the vegetables with the remaining olive oil.

Roast in the oven for 1½ hours. The turkey skin will crisp up while the inside will be cooked through and beautifully soft and juicy.

Serve on a large plate and garnish.

Chicken with Aromatic Red Rice

This is a dish introduced by Jewish immigrants from Iraq called t'bit, made by slow-cooking chicken in aromatic red rice. Each family has its own take on this dish. My old neighbour used to cook this and every time the wonderful aromas would waft through our window, making everyone hungry. It took me a while to fully replicate it, until I realized that cardamom was the missing ingredient that provided the dish's distinct flavour and aroma.

SERVES: 6–8

8–10 chicken drumsticks, skin-on

Salt and freshly ground black pepper, to season

2 tbsp olive oil

2 medium onions, diced

2 medium tomatoes, finely chopped

1 x 400g/14oz can of chopped tomatoes

4 garlic cloves, crushed

2 tbsp date molasses

2 tsp sweet paprika

1½ tsp baharat

4–5 cardamom pods, crushed

1½–2 tsp salt

Pinch of coarse ground black pepper

350g/12oz/2 cups basmati rice

240ml/9fl oz/1 cup water

Season the chicken generously with salt and pepper. Heat a little of the oil in a large saucepan on a medium-high heat. When hot, seal the chicken on both sides, then remove and set aside.

Wipe the pan clean (with paper towels), then sauté the onions on a medium heat in a splash of oil for 2–3 minutes until lightly golden. Push the onions to the side of the pan, add the fresh tomatoes and stir for about 3 minutes. Add the canned tomatoes and stir the onions back in. Cook for about 3 minutes, stirring occasionally. Add the garlic, date molasses, paprika, baharat, cardamom pods, salt and pepper. Mix well and let it cook for a few more minutes, then take the pan off the heat. Let it cool and transfer to a large bowl.

Rinse the rice in cold water until the water runs clear. Place in a medium pan with water and ½ teaspoon of salt, and bring to the boil on a high heat. Add the rice, give a quick stir, cover and let it cook for 5 minutes. Drain the rice through a colander and run the tap with cold water over it to stop the cooking process and get the remaining starch out. The rice will now be half-cooked, bright white, slightly tender, but will still have a bit of a bite. Add the rice to the bowl with the tomato sauce and mix well until combined.

In a large pan, spoon half the rice mixture, add the chicken on top, and then the rest of the rice to cover the chicken. Place the pan on a medium heat, make a little hole at the side of the rice and slowly add the water. Bring to the boil, then reduce the heat to very low. This is important otherwise the bottom will burn. When using a gas hob/stovetop, I like to use a SimmerMat heat diffuser underneath the saucepan to distribute the heat. Cover the lid with paper towels and simmer for 2–3 hours. The chicken will be falling off the bone.

Barberries

These small, ruby-coloured dried berries are grown around the world and are popular in the Middle East and Asia (particularly in Iran). They have a tangy flavour and are commonly used to add a sweet and sour taste to savoury dishes, or as an ingredient in desserts and jams. I truly love barberries for their delicate tangy kick, and use them generously on rice, salads, roasted vegetables and omelettes, as well as with meat and fish dishes. Keep them in the refrigerator to maintain their bright colour for longer.

Turkey Breast with Baharat & Grape Molasses

I love cooking turkey all year round. Its high protein level and low-fat content make it one of the healthiest and leanest meats. Because it's lean, I'm always extra careful not to overcook turkey so that it stays nice and moist. This recipe is an easy way to make sure it remains tender and full of flavour. The grape molasses has a deep, sweet flavour, but if you can't find it, it can be replaced with date molasses or honey. If you are like me, you will be making this dish again and again.

SERVES: 4

4 turkey breast fillets (or chicken)

2 tbsp rapeseed/canola
 or vegetable oil

For the marinade

2 tsp baharat

1½ tbsp grape molasses
 (or date molasses or honey)

3 garlic cloves, crushed

¾ tsp salt

6 tbsp olive oil

4 tbsp orange juice

½ tsp coarse ground black pepper

2 tbsp chopped parsley, plus
 an extra good pinch to serve

Wash and dry the turkey fillets.

In a large bowl, mix together the ingredients for the marinade, then place the turkey fillets in the marinade.

Place a griddle/grill pan (or frying pan) on a medium heat and brush with rapeseed/canola oil. When the pan is hot, add the turkey fillets and cook for about 2 minutes on each side. The fillets should have the griddle marks and turn a lovely golden colour. Make sure they're fully cooked but don't overcook them otherwise they'll get too dry.

Transfer the turkey fillets to a serving plate. Drizzle over the oil from the pan, then wipe the pan clean with paper towels and set it back on the heat. Pour the rest of the marinade into the hot pan and let it sizzle for 1 minute before pouring over the turkey.

Sprinkle with chopped parsley and serve.

Chicken with Olives & Raisins

My husband loves chicken, and this is certainly a household favourite. The combination of olives and raisins results in a delicate balance of sweet and savoury flavours. Once cooked, the chicken absorbs the sauce and gets slightly darker and very tender. I recommend serving it with white rice. I have made this dish probably more than any other, and it never disappoints.

SERVES: 6–8

1 tbsp olive oil

1 large onion, diced

6 garlic cloves, chopped

6 tbsp tomato purée/paste

1½ tbsp white wine vinegar

375ml/13fl oz/1½ cups water

1½ tsp ground cumin

1 tsp sweet paprika

½ tsp chilli flakes

8 skinless chicken thighs

150g/5½oz/1½ cups pitted
    green olives

200g/7oz/scant 1½ cups
    black raisins

Heat the olive oil in a medium-size, heavy saucepan over a medium heat. Sauté the onion for 2–3 minutes until translucent, then add the garlic for 1–2 minutes. Once the onion and garlic are slightly golden, add the tomato purée/paste, vinegar and water and give it a good mix. Add the cumin, paprika and chilli flakes. Increase the heat to high and bring to the boil.

Place the chicken in the sauce and let it continue to bubble for about 5 minutes.

Add the olives and raisins, bring back to the boil for a few more minutes, then reduce the heat to low, cover and simmer covered for 1½ hours. The chicken will be very tender and dark and will have absorbed the flavours. Serve with rice.

Za'atar & Pomegranate Molasses Chicken with Aubergine & Sour Cherries

This is a real Middle Eastern medley, with za'atar, pomegranate molasses, sour cherries and aubergine/eggplant being classic ingredients of the region. I love each ingredient on its own, so I've combined them into this punchy recipe. You can find sour cherries in Middle Eastern shops (either cans or frozen will do), but make sure you choose the pitted ones. This is a very practical dish because it's all baked in one pan with minimal mess.

SERVES: 6–8

2½ tbsp za'atar

1 tsp ras el hanout

½ tsp garlic salt

Pinch of salt

120ml/4fl oz/½ cup olive oil, plus an extra 3 tbsp for the pomegranate molasses glaze

2 aubergines/eggplants, cut into small cubes

10 banana shallots, cut in half or quarters, depending on size

10 mixed chicken thighs and drumsticks, skin-on

1 can of pitted sour cherries (drained weight 400g/14oz)

4 tbsp pomegranate molasses

Preheat the oven to 200ºC/400ºF/Gas 6.

In a small bowl, mix the za'atar, ras el hanout, garlic salt, salt and half the olive oil until combined.

Place the aubergines/eggplants and shallots in a large baking pan, drizzle with the remaining olive oil and add a pinch of salt and pepper, then mix well to coat the vegetables. Arrange the chicken in between the vegetables (make sure not too snugly) and brush the chicken with the za'atar mixture. Scatter over the sour cherries and cook in the oven for 50–55 minutes until the chicken skin is golden and crispy.

In a small bowl, mix the pomegranate molasses with the 3 tablespoons of olive oil.

When the chicken skin is golden and crispy, take the pan out of the oven, brush the chicken with the pomegranate molasses glaze, then place back in the oven for a further 15–20 minutes.

Serve straight to the table.

Slow-cooked Beef Cheeks with Dates & Pul Biber Chillies on a Bed of Creamy Polenta with Crispy Rosemary

This dish is comforting and luxurious at the same time. The beef cheeks are slow-cooked with a sweet and spicy sauce until they are soft and juicy. The creamy polenta/cornmeal complements the sweetness of the date molasses and the spiciness of the pul biber sauce. For me, polenta is the perfect carrier to showcase those flavours, but if you are not a polenta fan, you can replace it with another creamy mash of your choice or couscous.

SERVES: 4

3 tbsp rapeseed/canola or vegetable oil

1kg/2lb 4oz beef cheeks, cut into cubes

120g/4¼oz/scant 1 cup chopped pitted dates

4 garlic cloves, crushed

1½ tsp pul biber (Aleppo) chilli flakes

1½ tsp salt

1 tsp freshly ground black pepper

10 tbsp date molasses

6 tbsp honey

800ml/28fl oz/scant 3½ cups water

For the polenta

500ml/17fl oz/2 cups water

100g/3½oz/scant 1 cup polenta/cornmeal

½ tsp salt

100ml/3½fl oz/scant ½ cup oat milk

For the crispy rosemary

7–8 rosemary sprigs

120ml/4fl oz/½ cup rapeseed/canola or vegetable oil

Heat the oil in a large saucepan on a high heat. When hot, sear the beef cheeks on all sides. Once completely seared, take the beef cheeks out and set aside, leaving the oil in the pan.

Add the dates, garlic, chilli flakes, salt and pepper to the pan, give it a stir, then add the date molasses and honey. Mix for a few seconds, then add the water. Bring to the boil. Add the beef cheeks back to the pan and bring to the boil again, then reduce the heat and simmer, covered, for 2 hours until the meat is cooked and tender.

Take the lid off, give it a quick stir and cook, uncovered, for a further 20 minutes to thicken the sauce.

Meanwhile, make the polenta/cornmeal. In a medium saucepan, bring the water to the boil. Add the polenta and salt, stir, then add the oat milk. Bring to the boil again, then reduce the heat and simmer, covered, for 20–30 minutes.

For the crispy rosemary, first remove the rosemary leaves by pulling the leaves in the opposite direction from the stalk. Heat the oil in a small saucepan on a high heat. When hot, carefully add the rosemary and cook for a few seconds, then remove with a slotted spoon onto paper towels to absorb the excess oil.

When plating, spoon a generous amount of creamy polenta onto each plate, top with the beef cheeks, add an extra drizzle of the sauce, and sprinkle with the crispy rosemary.

Beef Stew with Dried Fruit & Dried Lime

Khoresh

Khoresh is an Iranian stew that's served with basmati rice and has many variations based around dried fruits, herbs and vegetables. I learnt to cook this type of stew from my father, who emigrated to Israel from Iran as a child. He wanted to preserve tastes from his home and, as he had a flare for cooking, he quickly learnt from his sisters how to make traditional Iranian dishes. He taught my mother, and they would make those special stews for Friday night meals. It's quite possibly our family's favourite food – it's definitely my sisters' and mine! This recipe has a strong flavour of dried fruit and dried lime, which appear frequently in Iranian kitchens. This unusual combination creates a rich, delicately balanced sweet and sour flavour. It's the first stew I learnt to cook and to this day, it transports me back to our Friday nights at home.

SERVES: 4–6

1 large onion, finely diced

Splash of rapeseed/canola or vegetable oil

500g/1lb 2oz cubed beef

375ml/13fl oz/1½ cups water

2 tbsp tomato purée/paste

2 tbsp plum jam (or any other red jam)

3 dried limes

90g/3¼oz/½ cup dried black-eyed beans, soaked in water overnight, or 200g/7oz canned black-eyed beans, drained and rinsed

15 dried apricots

15 prunes

1 tsp soft brown sugar

3 tbsp lemon juice

1 tsp salt

In a large saucepan on a medium heat, sauté the onion in a splash of oil for 3–4 minutes until golden.

Add the beef and let it brown and seal on all sides. Cover the meat with the water, bring to the boil and skim off and discard the foam that forms on top of the meat.

Mix the tomato purée/paste with 125ml/4fl oz/½ cup of water, then add to the saucepan. Repeat the same process with the jam. Mix everything well and bring to a gentle boil.

Break up the dried limes. They are quite hard so need to be crushed with a rolling pin, then you can break them up with your hands into 3–4 pieces each. Add to the pan along with the beans and dried fruit. Sprinkle in the sugar, add the lemon juice and season with the salt.

Cover with a lid and let it simmer for 2 hours, mixing occasionally.

When the khoresh is ready, it should be thick but liquid enough to serve over rice. If it's too thick, add a bit of water and cook for a further 30 minutes. If it's too watery, remove the lid and let it cook a little longer until it reduces and thickens to the required consistency. Serve with white basmati rice.

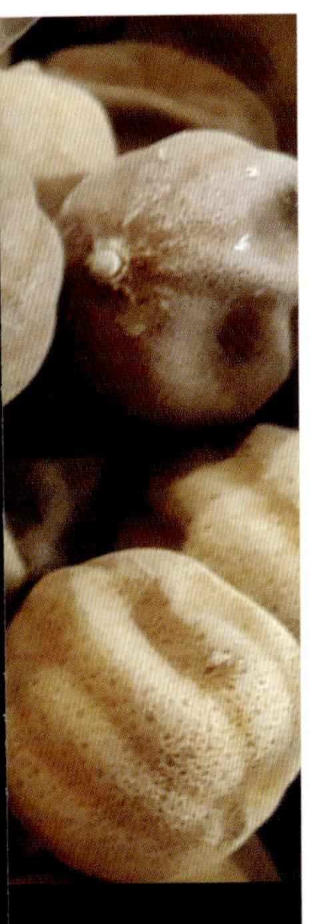

Dried Lime

Dried lime is possibly the most synonymous ingredient of Persian cuisine. The limes are extremely fragrant and have a very distinct tangy flavour. They are traditionally used in beef and lamb stews as well as soups and broths. I prefer to crack their skin open, exposing the dried pulp and seeds, before adding them to a dish, letting them cook until they soften and release their unique zesty flavour. They are generally available in dark and light colours; I always use the light-beige ones.

Khoresh Sabzi

Persian Herb Stew

Khoresh sabzi, or ghormeh gabzi, is a fragrant green stew full of herbs, cooked with red kidney beans and dried lime. It's considered one of Iranian cuisine's most iconic dishes, passed down through generations. My father taught my mum how to make various types of khoreshs (stews) and she used to cook the most exquisite sabzi, usually for Friday night dinner and always served with basmati rice. She appreciated its nutritional value, and we appreciated its delicious taste! The dried lime and dried fenugreek leaves are two ingredients that are important to create the distinct flavour; both can be found in Middle Eastern shops.

SERVES: 4

2 medium onions, diced

2 tbsp rapeseed/canola
    or vegetable oil

600g/1lb 5oz lamb, diced
    (can be made with beef)

½ tsp ground cumin

½ tsp ground coriander

90g/3¼oz/½ cup dried red kidney
    beans, soaked for at least 1 hour
    but preferably overnight, or ½
    x 400g/14oz can of red kidney
    beans, drained and rinsed

3 dried limes, crushed

½ tsp ground turmeric

Large bunch (150g/5½oz)
    of coriander/cilantro, finely
    chopped without the stalks
    (the herbs can be prepared
    in a food processor)

Large bunch (150g/5½oz)
    of parsley, finely chopped
    without the stalks

½ bunch (75g/2¾oz/2 cups)
    of mint leaves, finely chopped
    without the stalks

2 tbsp dried fenugreek

3 tsp soft brown sugar

1½ tsp salt

2 tbsp lemon juice

Sprinkle of sumac, to garnish

In a large saucepan, sauté 1 diced onion (keep the other for later) on a medium heat with a splash of the oil for 3–4 minutes. Once slightly golden, add the lamb and sear on all sides, stirring constantly. Add the cumin and coriander and mix for 2 minutes. Add enough water to cover the lamb by about 1cm/½in (about 1.5l/52fl oz/6½ cups) and bring to the boil. Add the beans and dried limes, then reduce the heat. Simmer for 1½–2 hours, covered, until the meat is tender, skimming off any foam from the top.

In a large frying pan, sauté the other onion on a medium heat with a splash of oil for about 3–4 minutes. Add the turmeric and stir for a further minute, then add all the chopped herbs. Turn down the heat to low and mix it all together, stirring occasionally until the herbs have wilted and turned a darker green, about 5 minutes. This is important because by doing this the herbs will create the unique flavour and texture for this dish.

Add the herbs to the saucepan with the meat. Add the dried fenugreek, sugar, salt and lemon juice. Simmer for another hour to allow the flavours to develop and the sauce to reduce.

Serve this green aromatic herby stew with white basmati rice and a sprinkle of sumac.

Dad's Koftas with Tahini & Pomegranate Seeds

My dad was a barbecue king back in the day, famous for his homemade kofta mix. As soon as summer started, he found any excuse to host abundant barbecues. Everything he grilled was made from scratch with aromatic flavours and cooked to perfection, but his koftas were the real star of the show. The kofta dish at Delamina is inspired by those famous barbecues. He never followed a recipe, so I had to make it a few times until I felt the flavours were close enough and I was happy for the chefs to prepare it. The lamb can be replaced with minced/ground beef.

MAKES: ABOUT 18 KOFTAS

For the koftas

500g/1lb 2oz minced/ground lamb

1 large onion, finely diced or grated

4 tbsp finely chopped coriander/cilantro

4 tbsp finely chopped parsley, plus extra for garnish

2 tbsp finely chopped dill

1½ tsp crushed garlic

½ tsp freshly ground black pepper

1 tsp ground turmeric

1 tsp ground cumin

1 tsp ground coriander

1 tsp ground cinnamon

1 tsp baharat

1½ tsp pul biber (Aleppo) chilli flakes

To serve

Tahini (see page 30)

3 tbsp extra virgin olive oil

Pul biber (Aleppo) chilli flakes

Pomegranate seeds

Chopped parsley

4 warm fluffy pitta bread, cut into quarters

3 tbsp roasted pine nuts (optional)

Place all the ingredients for the koftas in a large bowl and mix until well combined. This should be done preferably by hand as it's the best way to incorporate everything evenly together. (This can be done with gloves.)

Place a small plate with a bit of oil next to you while making the koftas.

Using a tablespoon, take some of the kofta mixture and shape it with your hands – first make a round shape, then flatten it out slightly. Dipping your fingers and palms in the oil from time to time will prevent the minced/ground meat mixture from sticking to your hands. Repeat until all the koftas are made.

Ideally cook the koftas on a barbecue, otherwise use a griddle/grill pan brushed with a splash of oil on a medium-high heat. When hot, cook the koftas for about 2 minutes on each side, or longer if you like your koftas well-done.

Spread some tahini on a serving plate with the back of a spoon, place the koftas on top, drizzle with the olive oil, then sprinkle with pul biber, pomegranate seeds, chopped parsley and pine nuts if you'd like. Scoop with warm pitta bread.

Vine Leaves Stuffed with Rice, Venison, Herbs & Dried Fruit

This is possibly my most heart-warming and nostalgic recipe, which is why I worked relentlessly to recreate it. This dish passed through generations of my father's family simply through watching and recreating, without ever being written down. Now, with that generation reaching their twilight years, I tried to get as many clues as I could, asking around and putting bits of information together. It all sounded like, "a bit of this with a bit of that and sometimes I add this and sometimes that", and of course no measurements. To my astonishment, the taste is always deliciously the same, but I wanted to create the closest written recipe that could be followed by anyone. It's certainly worth the effort! I prefer making these vine leaves with minced venison, as it's particularly lean and flavoursome, but it can be replaced with minced/ground beef or lamb.

MAKES: ABOUT 55–60 STUFFED VINE LEAVES

2 jars of vine leaves in brine, drained

500g/1lb 2oz minced/ground venison

500g/1lb 2oz risotto rice or
  pudding rice

80g/2¾oz/⅔ cup dried apricots,
  finely chopped

80g/2¾oz/⅔ cup dried prunes,
  finely chopped

3 tbsp finely chopped dill

3 tbsp finely chopped parsley

3 tbsp finely chopped coriander/
  cilantro

2 tsp salt

2 tsp ground turmeric

2 tsp ground cumin

1 tsp ground cinnamon

1 tsp dried fenugreek

2 large tomatoes, thinly sliced
  into circles

For the sauce

600ml/20fl oz/2½ cups water

2 tbsp tomato purée/paste

Juice of 1 lemon

3 tsp soft brown sugar

½ tsp salt

Place the vine leaves in a large bowl and cover with warm water. This softens them and takes away their bitterness. Leave to soak for about 20 minutes.

In a medium bowl, mix together the minced/ground venison and rice until combined. Add the dried fruit along with the chopped herbs, salt and spices and mix everything very well, preferably with your hands. This is the best way to incorporate all the ingredients evenly together. (This can be done with gloves.)

Arrange the sliced tomatoes in a large saucepan so they cover the base of the pan. This keeps the dish moist, adds flavour and prevents it from burning at the bottom.

For this part, you need a clean, flat surface and to be sitting comfortably. Take one vine leaf, place it flat on the surface in front of you with the top of the leaf pointing away from you and the base toward you. Take between a teaspoon or tablespoon of the venison filling, depending on the size of the leaf, and spoon it onto the vine leaf near the base. Fold the base of the leaf over the filling, then fold both sides of the leaf in. Roll it up and place inside the saucepan on top of the tomatoes. Continue making the stuffed vine leaves in this way and carefully place them at the bottom of the pan very close to each other to prevent them from opening. When you have a snug

layer, start the second layer on top and continue until all the mixture is used.

Mix the ingredients for the sauce in a large jug and pour over the vine leaves until they are completely covered. If needed, add more water to make sure they're all nicely covered. This is very important otherwise they will not cook properly and will stay hard and dry.

Cover the pan and place on a medium heat. Bring to the boil, then reduce the heat to very low and simmer for 3 hours until the vine leaves are soft inside. (When using a gas hob/stovetop, I like to use a SimmerMat heat diffuser underneath the saucepan to distribute the heat evenly.) Serve and enjoy.

שד בנימין אדמונד רוטשילד
ROTHSCHILD blvd.
רוטשילד 7
7
DA DA & DA

Sweet Things

My introduction to cooking was

through baking. My mother was a teacher and spent a large chunk of the day at work. She was, therefore, not a big believer in spending too much time making desserts, so I realized that if I wanted home-baked cakes, I must make them myself. (Having said that, as a grandmother, she became famous for her delicious apple crumble that she loved making for her grandchildren; it was my son's favourite.)

Very early on I liked to experiment with my sweet things – even if it was just a bar of chocolate, I'd grate it into a bowl, then scoop it up slowly with a teaspoon. The first cake I baked surprised me with how good it was, and from then on there was no turning back. Both my sisters were delighted, and my mother left me to my own devices, relieved to relinquish this role to me and allow me to play with my creations. Generally, it went well, except for once when I used the container of salt instead of sugar by mistake, and nearly threw up from the unexpected taste of flour, raw eggs, raw cocoa and salt! Other than that, I quite enjoyed it all.

Even today when creating recipes, it's desserts that I like working on the most. My philosophy at Delamina is the same as I have at home: to use high-quality ingredients that will shine; to use as little sugar as I can get away with without compromising on the flavour; and to substitute with healthier alternatives where possible. The same principles apply to butter: I reduce the amount or combine it with oil to maintain the delicate flavour but with a lighter feel. I also often use yogurt instead of cream. As I'm more of a savoury person, when eating sweets, they have to be particularly delightful and a little bit special. I hope you enjoy making and eating these.

Malebi with Rose Water, Raspberry Reduction & Pistachios

Malebi is a classic Middle Eastern dessert that's popular across the whole region. It's a particular favourite of my husband, who has fond memories of his grandfather bringing him malebi from a specific kiosk in Jaffa as a child. Nowadays, there are a few places that specialize in this lovely, creamy dessert, and you can choose from a selection of toppings that include nuts, cookies or a variety of different fruity syrups. Hamalebia is one of those cafes. It's a fun place to go for a sweet treat after a meal with friends and has an outdoor seating area where you can play a selection of board games on offer until the early hours of the morning. Traditional malebi is topped with a sugary red syrup, but in this recipe, I've replaced it with a raspberry reduction, to make it lighter and fresher.

MAKES: about 10 portions

1l/35fl oz/4¼ cups milk

280ml/9½fl oz/scant 1¼ cups whipping cream

100g/3½oz/½ cup caster/granulated sugar

4 tsp vanilla extract

3 tbsp rose water

120g/4¼oz/1 cup cornflour/cornstarch

For the raspberry reduction

150g/5½oz/1 cup frozen raspberries

100g/3½oz/½ cup caster/granulated sugar

150ml/5fl oz/⅔ cup water

1 tbsp lemon juice

2 tsp rose water

To serve

Chopped roasted pistachios

Edible rose petals (optional)

In a large bowl, mix all the ingredients except the cornflour/cornstarch, until combined. Put about 10 tablespoons of this mixture into another bowl and add the cornflour to it. Mix well.

Pour the mixture without the cornflour into a saucepan and place on a medium heat. When little bubbles start to appear at the edge of the pan, add the cornflour mixture and stir until it starts to thicken. At this point, give it a good last stir, remove from the heat, then pour into individual serving dishes. Place in the refrigerator for at least 2 hours until set.

Put all the ingredients for the raspberry coulis except the rose water into a saucepan on a medium heat. Bring to the boil, reduce the heat and simmer, uncovered, until it reduces by about half. This should take about 30 minutes. Add the rose water, remove from the heat and let it cool down completely.

Add a couple of spoonfuls of the coulis to each malebi and serve sprinkled with chopped pistachios and rose petals, if using.

Candied Peanut & Irish Cream Parfait

During one of my first visits to London as a young girl, I was surprised to learn that people eat ice cream in winter. As kids growing up in Tel Aviv, we only ate ice cream during the summer months – there wasn't an ice cream or ice lolly in sight during wintertime, so it was quite a revelation! That has also now changed in Tel Aviv, and with that in mind, Parfait is something I make and keep in the freezer all year round. Come rain or shine, for any occasion or season, it is always happily devoured by us or our guests.

SERVES: 10–12

3 egg whites

70g/2½oz/⅓ cup caster/
  granulated sugar

300ml/10½fl oz/1¼ cups
  whipping cream

1 tsp vanilla extract

2 tbsp Irish Cream liqueur

For the candied peanuts

100g/3½oz/1 cup unsalted peanuts

5 tbsp caster/granulated sugar

Pinch of salt

1½ tbsp water

Preheat the oven to 180°C/350°F/Gas 4 and line a baking tray with baking parchment.

For the candied peanuts, spread the peanuts out on the lined baking tray and roast in the oven for 10–12 minutes until lightly golden. Take them out and set aside to cool down. Transfer to a food processor and pulse lightly so they break up but don't turn to powder.

Into a medium-size saucepan on a medium-high heat, put the sugar, salt and water. Stir and watch how the sugar dissolves and the texture becomes syrupy and looks slightly golden. At this point, add the roasted peanuts and keep stirring constantly until well combined. Pour onto a sheet of baking parchment to cool down. Once cool, break into small pieces. Keep a few aside for decoration.

In a mixing bowl, beat the egg whites and sugar together using an electric mixer and keep beating until you get shiny stiff peaks.

In a separate bowl, with an electric mixer, whip the whipping cream with the vanilla extract and Irish Cream liqueur. Carefully fold the candied nuts into the whipped cream, then gently fold the stiff egg whites into the whipped cream until combined.

Line a container about 30 x 10cm/12 x 4in (or one that is 22 x 10cm/8½ x 4in will also work) with cling film/plastic wrap and pour in the parfait mixture. The cling film makes it easier to remove from the container before serving. Place in the freezer overnight.

When serving, cut the parfait into 1cm/½in slices. I like to lay two slices on top of each other, or sometimes cut them into triangles. Sprinkle with the reserved peanuts.

Grandma's Poppy Seed & Orange Cookies

My grandma's visits to Tel Aviv were always a special occasion for my sisters and me. She lived far away in a kibbutz, Ashdot Yaakov, near the Lake of Galilee, which meant she stayed with us for a few days. She always brought several large and colourful tins filled with delicious homemade cookies that we nicknamed (for obvious reasons) "salties" and "sweeties"; we enjoyed these long after she returned back home. During one of our visits to the kibbutz, she let me help her make these cookies. I remember entering this huge kitchen that catered for all 300 members of the community (kibbutzs are social communes where all meals are taken communally in a large dining hall); everything was super-sized, with huge pots and pans – I felt like a Lilliputian from Gulliver's Travels. It was special baking these cookies with her, and I cherish those memories. My favourite type was the poppy seed ones and although no one kept the recipe, I've tried to recreate them here and have come pretty close to the flavour and texture I loved so much.

MAKES: about 40 cookies

150g/5½oz unsalted butter

90g/3¼oz/½ cup soft brown sugar

3 tbsp fresh orange juice

2 tbsp vegetable oil

1 tsp orange zest

1 tsp vanilla extract

1 egg

300g/10½oz/2 cups plain/
  all-purpose flour

1 tsp baking powder

2 tbsp poppy seeds

2 tbsp soft brown sugar, for rolling

Preheat the oven to 160°C/320°F/Gas 3½ and line a large baking tray with baking parchment.

In a large bowl, beat the butter and sugar with an electric mixer until light and fluffy. Add the orange juice, oil, orange zest, vanilla and egg and mix again until well combined.

In a separate bowl, mix the flour and baking powder.

Add the flour to the butter and orange mixture and combine, then add the poppy seeds and mix one more time. Cover with cling film/plastic wrap and chill in the refrigerator for 1 hour.

Take half the amount and roll with your hands into a cylinder/log shape about 5cm/2in wide.

Sprinkle the brown sugar on the lined baking tray and roll the cookie dough in the sugar. Using a sharp knife, slice the dough into cookies 5mm/¼in thick. Spread them out on the baking tray. Repeat with the second half of the cookie mix.

Bake in the oven for 20–25 minutes until they are golden brown all over. Let them cool for a few minutes and then enjoy or store in an airtight container.

Apple & Plum Crumble

This was my mum's favourite dessert to make, and my kids would devour it in minutes when she made it. It's easy to pull together and so satisfying. When I started making this crumble myself, I experimented with various types of fruit and found that the apple and plum combination had the perfect balance of sweet and sour, although you can make it with just apples or plums. It can be served with vanilla ice cream or on its own.

SERVES: 6–8

200g/7oz/1¼ cups plain/all-purpose flour (can be gluten-free)

50g/1¾oz/½ cup ground almonds

100g/3½oz/½ cup soft brown sugar

100g/3½oz cold unsalted butter, cubed

3 Granny Smith eating apples, peeled, cored and thinly sliced

3 Bramley cooking/baking apples, peeled, cored and thinly sliced

4–5 medium red plums, pitted and thinly sliced

½ tsp ground cinnamon

Preheat the oven to 180°C/350°F/Gas 4.

In a large bowl, mix the flour, ground almonds and sugar together. Add the butter and rub it in with your fingertips until it looks like breadcrumbs. (This can be done with gloves.)

Arrange about half of the apples (both types) to cover the bottom of an ovenproof dish (approx. 25 x 33cm/10 x 13in), then top with a layer of all the plums, followed by another layer of the remaining apples.

Sprinkle the top layer of apples with the cinnamon, then sprinkle the crumble evenly on top. (Don't press it down; let it stay fluffy and loose.)

Bake in the oven for 50 minutes until golden and the edges are caramelized.

Serve with vanilla ice cream or on its own.

Meringue with Orange Blossom Mousse, Raspberry Coulis, Mixed Berries & Pomegranate Seeds

This crowd-pleasing light dessert is easy to make, quick to assemble and absolutely delicious! If you prefer, there are some good ready-made meringues you can buy, which makes this even simpler to put together. I include as many types of berries as I can get my hands on, and pomegranate seeds to add crunch and zest. Don't be tempted to skip the orange blossom water; its flavour is subtle but gives an exotic aroma you don't want to miss. I must have made this dessert more than any other! I hope it serves you well.

SERVES: 10

For the meringue

4 egg whites, at room temperature

100g/3½oz/½ cup caster/granulated sugar

100g/3½oz/scant ¾ cup icing/confectioners' sugar

For the raspberry mix

50g/1¾oz/⅓ cup frozen raspberries

1½ tsp (5g/⅛ oz) icing/confectioners' sugar

For the orange blossom mousse

260ml/8¾fl oz/1 cup whipping cream

40g/1½oz/⅓ cup icing/confectioners' sugar

1 tsp orange blossom water

For the raspberry coulis

120g/4¼oz/scant 1 cup frozen raspberries

50g/1¾oz/¼ cup caster/granulated sugar

1 tbsp lemon juice

To serve

75g/2¾oz/½ cup raspberries

75g/2¾oz/½ cup blueberries

75g/2¾oz/½ cup blackberries

75g/2¾oz/½ cup strawberries, sliced into quarters

2 tbsp pomegranate seeds

Mint leaves (optional)

Preheat the oven to 100°C/215°F/Gas ¼.

To make the meringue, in a large bowl, whisk the egg whites and caster/granulated sugar with an electric mixer and once the foam is beginning to form, slowly add the icing/confectioners' sugar and whisk for about 5 more minutes until the mixture becomes glossy and you get very stiff peaks.

Using a large spoon, scoop up some of the meringue mixture and slide it onto a baking parchment-lined baking tray with the help of another spoon; you'll have about 10 dollops. Bake for 2 hours until crisp on the outside but soft in the middle. Take out of the oven and let them cool.

To make the raspberry mix, defrost the frozen raspberries in a small saucepan over a very low heat (or defrost at room temperature for 1 hour before). Mix in the icing sugar and set aside to cool down.

In a large bowl, whip the whipping cream, the raspberry mix, icing sugar and orange blossom water with an electric mixer until you get stiff peaks.

Put the ingredients for the raspberry coulis in a small saucepan and cook on a low heat for a few minutes until combined.

Break up the meringues onto your serving plates. Spoon over the mousse and gently mix together. To serve, scatter the washed mixed berries and pomegranate seeds on top and drizzle with the raspberry coulis. Sprinkle over mint leaves, if desired.

Orange Blossom & Rose Water

The cuisine of the Eastern Mediterranean uses two ingredients that have perfume-like properties and add a dash of magic to dishes.

ROSE WATER

This fragrant water, infused with rose petals, is used throughout the Middle East to enhance desserts and drinks. It is very potent, and a small amount makes a big impact. It's often used in beauty and scented products and has antioxidant properties. I also love using the beautiful pink rose petals to decorate desserts.

ORANGE BLOSSOM

This is my all-time favourite scent and hence I chose the orange blossom flower to be illustrated on the cover of this book. Water infused with orange blossom petals is used in the same way as rose water, but gives a more subtle fragrance and delicate aroma to desserts and drinks. It has also been used for centuries in perfumes and ancient medicine for its therapeutic properties.

Chocolate & Coffee Cake with Coffee Mousse Topping

Personally, I like my chocolate cakes rich in flavour without being too heavy. This chocolate cake has a subtle coffee flavour, and the light and airy mousse topping is so delicious I could eat it on its own with a spoon! The mousse should ideally be in the refrigerator for 2 hours before it's whipped up, so it's important to start making it first. Then by the time the cake is prepared, baked and cooled down, it will be ready to spread. (Alternatively, it can be made the night before.) I like to finish the cake by decorating it with crushed rose petals for their vivid colour and pleasant aroma.

SERVES: 20

3 tbsp unsweetened cocoa powder

3 tsp instant coffee

100g/3½oz/½ cup soft brown sugar

240ml/9fl oz/1 cup milk

100g/3½oz dark/bittersweet chocolate

150g/5½oz unsalted butter, cut into cubes, plus extra for greasing

2 tbsp vegetable oil

5 eggs (medium)

240g/8½oz/1½ cups self-raising/self-rising flour

200g/7oz/1 cup caster/granulated sugar

Crushed dried rose petals and dried rose buds, to decorate

For the coffee mousse topping

250ml/9fl oz/1 cup whipping cream, plus 4 tbsp to dissolve the coffee

2 tbsp instant coffee

250ml double/heavy cream

60g/2¼oz milk chocolate

140g/5oz white chocolate

See page 174

Start with the mousse topping, as it needs to chill in the refrigerator for 2 hours while you prepare and bake the cake. Place 4 tablespoons of the whipping cream in a little bowl, add the instant coffee, then set it aside to dissolve.

Pour the cream into a small saucepan over a low heat and let it slowly heat for about 3 minutes.

Into a medium-size, heatproof bowl, break up the milk and white chocolates.

When small bubbles start to appear at the edge of the cream in the saucepan, stir for a minute or 2 more, then pour it over the chocolate. Mix well until the chocolate melts completely. Once combined, add the cream with the coffee, mix and stir until completely smooth. Chill in the refrigerator for 2 hours. This stage can also be done the night before.

Preheat the oven to 160°C/320°F/Gas 3½ and grease two 23cm/9in round cake pans.

Place a small saucepan on a medium heat with the cocoa powder, instant coffee, brown sugar and milk, and heat while stirring. When the mixture is warm, break up the chocolate into pieces and add to the pan while constantly stirring.

Take the pan off the heat and add the butter. Keep stirring until the butter has completely melted, then add the oil and give it a last stir.

Separate the egg whites and yolks. Add the yolks to the chocolate mixture and stir until thick and smooth. Add the flour and mix until well combined.

In a large bowl, whisk the whites with an electric hand whisk/beater on a medium-high speed and slowly add the caster/granulated sugar until you get glossy stiff peaks. Fold carefully into the chocolate batter.

Pour the batter into the two prepared cake pans, dividing it evenly, and then bake in the oven for 25–30 minutes, or until a cocktail stick/toothpick inserted into the middle comes out dry. Turn the cakes out onto a wire/cooling rack to leave to cool down.

Remove the mousse from the refrigerator and add the remaining whipping cream. Use an electric hand whisk on a low-medium speed and beat for about 1½–2 minutes, until a silky, firm mousse forms. (Don't be tempted to put the mixer on a higher speed because the mousse will split. Also, be sure to stop when the mousse is firm so it doesn't lose its texture.)

When the cakes are completely cool, evenly spread (or pipe) the mousse over the cakes and place one on top of the other, sprinkle with crushed rose petals and rose buds to decorate and enjoy.

Nectarine Summer Cake

I love making this cake. Almost everything just goes into one bowl and then all you do is place it in the oven – and done! In this recipe, I use nectarines, but you can also use other fruit, such as raspberries or plums, depending on the season. I also find that coconut sugar gives the final flavour a slight caramel twist, while the yogurt keeps it light and fresh. It's nice to serve with crème fraîche but it's just as tasty on its own.

SERVES: 16

2 eggs

200g/7oz/¾ cup plain yogurt

1 tsp vanilla extract

50g/1¾oz butter, melted,
  plus extra for greasing

5 tbsp vegetable oil

210g/7½oz/scant 1½ cups
  self-raising/self-rising flour

180g/6¼oz/1¼ cups coconut sugar

Pinch of salt

For the nectarine syrup

6 tbsp water

2½ tbsp soft brown sugar

1½ tbsp lemon or lime juice

2 large nectarines (or 3 small
  ones), pitted and thinly sliced
  (3–4mm/⅛in thick)

For the crème fraîche

150ml/5fl oz/⅔ cup crème fraîche

2 tsp icing/confectioners' sugar

1 tbsp nectarine syrup
  (from above)

See page 175

Preheat the oven to 180ºC/350ºF/Gas 4 and grease a 20cm/8in round cake pan.

First make the nectarine syrup. Place a small saucepan on a medium heat with the water, brown sugar and lemon juice. Bring to the boil and stir to dissolve the sugar, then add the nectarines. Bring back to the boil, then reduce the heat and simmer for 10 minutes. Set aside and let the nectarines soak up the syrup while you make the cake.

In a medium bowl, beat the eggs with a fork for 1 minute, add the yogurt and beat together for another minute until there are no lumps, then add the vanilla extract, melted butter and oil and stir until well combined.

In a separate large bowl, mix the flour, coconut sugar and salt. Pour in the yogurt mixture and combine. Add the nectarine slices (keep the syrup aside) and mix.

Pour the batter into the prepared cake pan and spread level. Bake in the oven for 45 minutes, then check that a cocktail stick/toothpick inserted into the middle comes out dry.

Mix the crème fraîche with the icing/confectioners' sugar and nectarine syrup until well combined and serve with the cake.

Kadayif Nest of Vanilla Cheesecake Cream with Caramelized Pecans & Orange Peel Syrup

This elegant and moreish dessert never fails to turn heads and was inevitably the first dessert I placed on the menu at Delamina, where it became an immediate hit. I fell in love with it years ago at my first boyfriend's house one summer afternoon when we found a tray filled to the brim with these crispy thin noodles topped with a divine cream cheese that was so light and creamy. His mother caught us red-handed with an almost empty tray and embarrassed faces. I wanted to capture the lightness of this dessert, so I initially made it with fat-free cheese, although that became hard to source. It later evolved into a recipe using light cream cheese and ricotta, which is airy yet wonderfully cheesy and moreish. Each step in this recipe is necessary to capture the balance of textures and flavours which make this dessert so popular. The kadayif noodles can be found in Middle Eastern shops.

SERVES: 6

For the kadayif noodles

150g/5½oz kadayif noodles, defrosted if you buy them frozen

1½ tbsp melted butter

1½ tbsp vegetable oil

1½ tbsp icing/confectioners' sugar

For the vanilla cheesecake cream

200g/7oz light Philadelphia cream cheese

100g/3½oz ricotta cheese

200ml/7fl oz/scant 1 cup double/heavy cream

3 tsp vanilla extract

10 tbsp icing/confectioners' sugar

6 tsp lemon juice

For the caramelized pecans

100g/3½oz/scant 1 cup pecans

80g/2¾oz/scant ½ cup caster/granulated sugar

250ml/9fl oz/1 cup water

3–4 tbsp rapeseed/canola or vegetable oil

For the orange peel syrup

3 oranges

200g/7oz/1 cup caster/granulated sugar

500ml/17fl oz/2 cups water

The orange peel syrup can be made in advance. To make the syrup, wash the oranges well and peel them. Place the peels in a small saucepan, add the sugar and water. Bring to the boil, then reduce the heat to very low, cover and simmer for about 1 hour until it becomes thick and syrupy and full of flavour. Discard the peels. Leave the syrup to cool. You can keep the syrup in the refrigerator for a few weeks.

When you want to make the complete recipe, preheat the oven to 180°C/350°F/Gas 4.

Place the noodles on a baking parchment-lined baking tray and separate them out with your hands by gently pulling them apart, without breaking them.

Mix the butter, oil and icing/confectioners' sugar until well combined, then drizzle over the noodles. With your hands, toss and pull the noodles until coated with the sugary mix. Divide the noodles into six equal portions and form each one into a nest-like shape.

Bake in the oven for about 13–15 minutes until golden. Remove and set aside to cool.

Next, make the cheesecake cream. In a large bowl, mix the cream cheese and ricotta until just combined. Add the cream, vanilla, icing sugar and lemon juice. With an electric hand whisk/beater, whisk on a low-medium speed for about a minute until the mixture

See page 181

thickens and becomes nice and smooth. Place in the refrigerator for 30 minutes minimum, or until you assemble.

Meanwhile, make the caramelized pecans. Place the pecans, caster/granulated sugar and water in a small saucepan on a medium heat and bring to the boil. Reduce the heat to low and simmer, uncovered, for about 20 minutes, or until the liquid thickens and becomes syrupy. Drain the pecans and place on a flat surface to cool down.

Heat the oil in a frying pan on a medium-high heat and fry the pecans until they become slightly darker and shiny. Keep an eye on them as they shouldn't get too dark, otherwise they will become bitter.

Remove the pecans from the pan and set aside to cool. They will last for 4 weeks.

To assemble, place one dollop of the cheesecake cream mixture into each kadayif nest, sprinkle with the caramelized pecans and drizzle with the orange peel syrup.

Mousse of Cherries & Raw Tahini with Pistachio Sprinkle

This dish was born from a childhood treat I used to love. When Tel Aviv was young, the main street at the heart of the city was called Dizengoff, named after the first mayor of Tel Aviv. Dizengoff Street, which is situated 10 minutes from the beach, is still bustling with life today, full of restaurants, cafes and trendy shops. But years ago, I knew it best for the tiny ice-cream shop that produced one of the most delicious combinations I have ever tasted, before the days of countless bases and toppings. This ice cream was vanilla with fresh fruit and whipped cream topped with cherries. I used to go there often, and since then I have always had a soft spot for cherries, incorporating them into some of my desserts. This particular dessert combines Amarena cherries with raw tahini, creating a sweet and slightly nutty flavour with a sour edge. A great way to end any meal!

SERVES: 4

2 tsp raw tahini

1 tsp runny honey

1 tsp vanilla extract

300ml/10½fl oz/1¼ cups whipping cream

60g/2¼oz amarena cherries in syrup, drained and cut into quarters, or smaller pieces if you prefer

1 tbsp amarena cherry syrup

50g/1¾oz/⅓ cup pistachios

Mix the tahini, honey and vanilla extract in a medium-size, heatproof bowl.

Heat half the whipping cream in a saucepan on a low heat until warm but not reaching boiling point, stirring constantly.

Slowly pour the warm cream into the bowl with the tahini mixture and stir well. Add the chopped cherries and the cherry syrup and mix until well combined. Set aside to cool down a little, then put into the refrigerator for 1 hour.

Add the remaining whipping cream to the mix and lightly whisk using an electric hand whisk/beater on low until it thickens. Put back in the refrigerator for at least a couple of hours.

Preheat the oven to 180°C/350°F/Gas 4.

Spread the pistachios out on a baking sheet and roast in the oven for 15 minutes. When done, take them out and set aside to cool down. Once cool, roughly chop the nuts or use a pestle and mortar to roughly crush them.

When you are ready to serve, spoon the desired amount of mousse onto individual dessert plates and sprinkle with the pistachios.

Banana, Pecan & Date Cake

Bananas, pecans and dates always take me back to my childhood. My mum's kibbutz, Ashdot Yaakov, is situated by the lake of Galilee and enjoys hot weather year-round, meaning it has perfect conditions for its abundant banana trees, pecan orchards and impressive date-palm fields. One of my fondest childhood memories in the kibbutz is gathering pecans, cracking them open all afternoon with my sisters and enjoying their delicious flavour. Sometimes my uncle would take me on an adventure to see the dates being harvested. I would be raised up in a crane and watch it all from up close. This cake always puts me in a good mood.

SERVES: 10–12

80g/2¾oz unsalted butter, plus extra for greasing

150g/5½oz/¾ cup soft brown sugar

2 eggs, beaten

240g/8½oz/2 cups self-raising/ self-rising flour (gluten-free flour also works)

½ tsp salt

60ml/2fl oz/¼ cup milk (I use oat milk, but any will do)

1 tbsp date molasses

3 ripe bananas, mashed well with a fork

80g/2¾oz pecans, broken into pieces

2 dates, pitted and chopped into small pieces

For decoration (optional)

Thin slices of banana and a few pecans

Preheat the oven to 180°C/350°F/Gas 4 and grease a loaf pan (11 x 21cm/4½ x 8½in).

Melt the butter. I suggest doing this either in a small saucepan on a very low heat or in a microwave on a low setting. Once the butter begins to melt, turn off the heat and stir until it is melted completely. Pour into a mixing bowl.

Add the sugar and beaten eggs to the melted butter and mix well.

Add the flour and mix again. Then add and mix one by one the salt, milk, date molasses, bananas and finally the pecans and dates.

Pour the mixture into the greased loaf pan and spread level, then add some thin slices of banana on top and sprinkle over a few pecans, if using.

Bake in the oven for about 40–45 minutes. Check if it's ready by inserting a cocktail stick/toothpick into the cake; it should come out almost dry.

Drinks

I've never been keen on a big breakfast first thing in the morning and instead prefer to have a smoothie or shake. They're quick and easy to make, versatile and can be packed with nutritious ingredients like fruit, seeds, nuts, herbs and spices. Also, when my kids were teenagers, always having to rush to school, I found that making a shake was a great way to give them a shot of goodness on the go. (It was also a reminder of a delicious fruit shake my mum used to make for them as young children.) I could easily add other particularly nutritious ingredients such as chia seeds, maca powder, flaxseeds and goji berries. One of the treats of visiting Tel Aviv is the many juice bars scattered around with a plethora of fruit on display, superfoods in jars, and unusual recipe combinations. We always start our mornings with a visit to our local juice bar, Tamara, a circular kiosk with glorious bright fruit hanging all around that makes an endless combination of freshly squeezed juices and smoothies.

When using chia seeds and flaxseeds, I strongly recommend the milled form, either crushed in the blender at home or purchased that way. This is the most beneficial way to eat them, as we can more easily access their nutrients. Whole chia seeds can be left overnight in water to become jelly-like in texture, making them easier to digest, although I prefer them milled when adding to shakes. In terms of liquids, the choice is varied. My preference is oat milk, sometimes diluted with water, but you can use cow's milk or any milk alternatives.

In this section, you'll find a wide selection of smoothies with variations of healthy ingredients and superfoods: ginger, turmeric, cinnamon, walnuts, almonds, avocados, raw cocoa powder and so on. I hope you'll enjoy them and feel adventurous to make your own combinations. Some of the best smoothies I've made have come about from using random ingredients I had in the refrigerator.

I've also added a few drinks that I often make to have with meals or for after. Limonana and infused teas are served everywhere in Tel Aviv and are very popular at our Delaminas.

Raspberry, Banana & Chia Seed Shake

Sweet, filling but not too heavy. This is a good morning pick-me-up that always puts a smile on my face. It's important to use ripe bananas (they're best when a few black dots start to appear on the skin) as they give the sweetness and right texture to the drink. You can mix and match with the berries you prefer, but I don't like to use blueberries as they can make the shake very thick, and if you leave it for a few minutes it becomes too thick to drink.

SERVES: 2

½ cup ice cubes

7–8 raspberries

1 ripe banana, peeled and sliced

4–5 strawberries

1 tsp milled chia seeds

1 tsp milled flaxseeds

2 pitted dates

200ml/7fl oz/scant 1 cup oat milk

100ml/3½fl oz/scant ½ cup water

Place all the ingredients in a blender and blitz until smooth.

Pour into glasses to serve.

Cucumber, Mint, Ginger & Turmeric Shake

This lovely fresh shake is full of nutrients. Turmeric is known for its nutritional properties, so I like to use it whenever possible. Here I've combined it with ginger, almonds, mint and cucumber to create a refreshing and healthy drink. It is water-based so is particularly light, and the almonds give it a creamy texture.

SERVES: 2

½ cup ice cubes

½ large cucumber

Leaves from 4 mint sprigs

Thumb-size piece of root ginger, peeled

Juice of ½ lemon

⅓ tsp ground turmeric

50g/1¾oz/¼ cup almonds

3 tsp honey

200ml/7fl oz/scant 1 cup water

Place all the ingredients in a blender and blitz until smooth.

Pour into glasses to serve.

Goji Berry, Apple, Walnut & Cinnamon Shake

This is our family go-to shake. With its sweetness coming solely from the fruit and goji berries, it's a winner on all fronts – healthy and tasty – and with the apple and cinnamon combination, I can only describe it as a guilt-free apple strudel.

SERVES: 2

½ cup ice cubes

3 tbsp dried goji berries

1 medium eating apple, cored and chopped

25g/1oz/¼ cup walnuts

1 tsp milled chia seeds

½ tsp ground cinnamon

200ml/7fl oz/scant 1 cup oat milk

50ml/2fl oz/¼ cup water

Place all the ingredients in a blender and blitz until smooth.

Pour into glasses to serve.

Avocado & Cocoa Shake

This is my healthy version of a chocolate milkshake. It's packed with goodness, and the raw cocoa powder combined with the avocado creates a delicious creamy texture. For a sweeter chocolaty taste, you can increase the amount of cocoa and agave. Sprinkling grated chocolate on top is a great way to add texture.

SERVES: 2

½ cup ice cubes

½ small avocado, peeled and pitted

12g/½oz/½ cup baby spinach, washed

3 tsp cocoa powder

2 tbsp dried goji berries

1 tsp milled chia seeds

1 tsp maca powder (optional)

3 tsp light agave syrup or honey

250ml/9fl oz/1 cup oat milk

100ml/3½fl oz/scant ½ cup water

1 tbsp grated dark/bittersweet chocolate, to garnish (optional)

Place all the ingredients (except the grated chocolate) in a blender and blitz until smooth.

Pour into glasses to serve. Sprinkle with the grated chocolate, if using.

See page 190 for all recipes

Limonana

The word "Limonana" is a comination of lemon and nana, which means "mint" in Hebrew – so you can guess the flavour of this drink! It's the most refreshing combination on a hot summer's day. You'll find it in most cafes and restaurants in Tel Aviv or anywhere along the beach. In some restaurants, you'll even get it as a welcome drink in a jug.

MAKES: 1 SMALL JUG OR 2 LARGE GLASSES

4 tsp caster/granulated sugar
80ml/2¾fl oz/⅓ cup hot water
2 cups ice cubes
Juice of 1 lemon
Leaves from 3–4 mint sprigs
1 tsp agave syrup

See page 191

Firstly, dissolve the sugar in the hot water, mix well and leave aside to cool.

Put all the ingredients, including the sugar water, into a blender and give it a few pulses to crush the ice and break up the mint leaves. Don't blitz it too much.

Pour into a small jug or divide between two glasses and enjoy.

Mint Tea with Cinnamon & Rose Water

Drinking this tea always transports me to Marrakesh where I first tried tea with rose water. Only a touch of rose water is needed to create the lovely aroma. If I have guests, I usually make it in one large teapot and serve it in little mugs. Every time you pour, the scent of mint, cinnamon and rose water fills the air.

SERVES: 4-6

1l/35fl oz/4¼ cups boiling water
8–10 mint sprigs
2 cinnamon sticks
1 English breakfast teabag
¼ tsp rose water
3–4 tsp honey

Pour the boiling water into a large teapot, then add the mint and cinnamon sticks to infuse.

Dip in the teabag for about 5–6 seconds only, to impart some colour and a little flavour, but not to overpower the other ingredients. Add the rose water and honey, give it a good stir until the honey completely dissolves, and enjoy.

Cupboard Essentials

Olive Mix

We love our olives in Tel Aviv and you'll often be given a generous plate of olives when seated at a restaurant. Many of the city's delicatessens offer a wide range of olives, and you can almost lose yourself among the different varieties. This mix uses the flavours of the region. I make sure we always have some in the refrigerator at home.

750g/1lb 10oz/12 cups green olives (I prefer nocellara)

1 lemon, washed well and sliced into small triangles (with the peel on)

10g/¼oz/⅓ cup dill, washed and roughly chopped

4 thyme sprigs, washed and each sprig cut in half

10g/¼oz/⅓ cup parsley, washed and roughly chopped without the stalks

1 tsp cumin seeds

1 tsp coriander seeds

1 red chilli, washed, half the seeds removed and finely sliced into circles

80ml/2¾fl oz/⅓ cup olive oil

200ml/7fl oz/scant 1 cup olive brine

Juice of 1 lemon

Place the olives in a large bowl. Add the rest of the ingredients and mix well.

Transfer to a large container with a lid and keep in the refrigerator. They should keep for a few weeks.

Dukkah

This is an aromatic mix of roasted nuts and seeds that originated in Egypt and is now popular across the Middle East. Typically used as a dip with bread or pitta bread, it can be sprinkled on vegetables and salads, adding flavour, crunchiness and an exotic Middle Eastern aroma to almost anything you want.

50g/1¾oz/⅓ cup blanched almonds

40g/1½oz hazelnuts

20g/¾oz pistachios

10g/¼oz/1 tbsp sesame seeds

25g/1oz/2½ tbsp pumpkin seeds

1 tbsp coriander seeds

2 tsp cumin seeds

½ tsp salt

Pinch of coarse ground
  black pepper

1 tsp sweet paprika

See page 201

Preheat the oven to 180°C/350°F/Gas 4.

Spread out the almonds, hazelnuts and pistachios on a baking sheet in one layer. Roast in the oven for 11–12 minutes until they get a very slight colour and release a delicate aroma. Make sure you don't leave them longer otherwise they'll become bitter. Set aside to cool down and crisp up.

Place a small frying pan on a low heat and dry-fry the sesame seeds for just a few minutes until they turn golden, stirring constantly so they don't burn and they roast evenly. Set aside to cool down. Do the same with the pumpkin seeds and set aside.

Put the pan back on the heat and turn the heat to medium. When the pan is hot, dry-fry, one after the other, the coriander seeds for about 1 minute, then the cumin seeds for about 30–40 seconds, or until they pop. Transfer to a small, heatproof bowl to cool down.

Use a pestle and mortar to crush (in batches, if needed) the almonds, hazelnuts, pistachios, pumpkin seeds, and coriander and cumin seeds, then transfer to a medium bowl. Add the roasted sesame seeds, the salt, pepper and paprika and mix together.

Alternatively, you can put everything except the sesame seeds and paprika into a food processor with the salt and pepper, and pulse until they are finely crushed but not too much. Be careful not to over-blend as the nuts and seeds will release their oil and can become a paste. It should be a dry mixture. Add the roasted sesame seeds and paprika at the end.

Transfer the dukkah to a jar and preferably keep in the refrigerator. It will keep for a few weeks.

Roasted Sweet Almond Spread

I'm transported back to Marrakesh every time I make this dip. The argan oil, made from the kernels of the argan tree, is widely used in Morocco. It's a delicate oil with a subtle, nutty flavour and is renowned for its nutritional properties. This is a wonderful treat to have ready in the refrigerator. It can be used either as a spread on its own, or with a fruity granola or yogurt. (If you can't find argan oil, use light olive oil instead. Do not replace with extra virgin olive oil, as its flavour is too strong.)

80g/2¾oz almonds
6 tbsp argan oil (or light olive oil)
4 tsp honey
2 tsp date molasses

See page 201

Preheat the oven to 180°C/350°F/Gas 4.

Spread the almonds out on a baking sheet and roast in the oven for 10–12 minutes.

Transfer the roasted almonds to a food processor. Add the oil, honey and date molasses and blitz until it becomes a thick, grainy paste. It takes a few minutes to achieve this consistency.

Transfer to a glass jar and keep in the refrigerator. It will keep for about 10 days.

Apricot & Orange Blossom Preserve

I've adored apricots ever since I was a little girl, when my mum introduced me to "Leder", a roll of pressed dried apricots. It was just the right balance of sweet and sour, every bite truly divine. Unfortunately, apricots only have a short season at the beginning of summer, but making this homemade apricot preserve is a way to prolong their season just a little longer. Pairing it with orange blossom water enhances the aroma and delicate flavour. (As this preserve is homemade with much less sugar than store-bought ones, it is best to keep it in the refrigerator and consume within a few weeks. Therefore, I divide it into a few small containers and keep some in the freezer, so it lasts longer.)

800g/1lb 12oz apricots

150g/5½oz/¾cup caster/
  granulated sugar

4 tbsp lemon juice

120ml/4fl oz/½ cup water

1 tsp orange blossom water

Wash the apricots, cut them in half and discard the stones, then slice into quarters.

Place a small, heavy saucepan on a low-medium heat, put the apricots in the pan and sprinkle the sugar on top. Add the lemon juice and water, mix and bring to the boil. Reduce the heat to low, cover and simmer for 30 minutes, mixing occasionally. Take the lid off, add the orange blossom water, stir and let it simmer for a further 20–25 minutes until it thickens up.

Set aside to let it cool down completely before transferring to sterilized, airtight containers. Keep in the refrigerator for 10–14 days or in the freezer for up to 3 months.

Black Grape & Chia Seed Preserve

I have such fond memories from the period of my childhood that I spent at my grandmother's kibbutz, Ashdot Yaakov. I have always been very close to my family there. The tradition in the kibbutzim is that main meals are eaten in the hall, but when snacking at her place, I would immediately scour the refrigerator for a jar of black grape jam. This was a speciality of my grandmother's sister, who was an exceptional cook. This recipe is a humble nod to the best jam I've ever tasted. Maybe part of the reason I remember the flavour so fondly was because I ate it surrounded by my close family.

500g/1lb 2oz seedless black grapes, washed and cut in half

1 medium apple (120g/4¼oz) peeled, cored and chopped

80g/2¾oz/scant ½ cup caster/granulated sugar

1½ tbsp lemon juice

2 tsp date molasses

1 tsp chia seeds

See page 205

In a medium-size, heavy saucepan, place the halved grapes and the chopped pieces of apple.

Place the pan on a medium heat and sprinkle the sugar on top. Watch how the sugar dissolves and stir.

Add the lemon juice, date molasses and chia seeds and bring to the boil, stirring constantly. Reduce the heat and simmer for 30 minutes.

Set aside to let it cool down completely before transferring to an airtight container. Keep in the refrigerator for 10–14 days or in the freezer for up to 3 months.

Red Onion & Sumac Pickle

This vibrant onion pickle is a great addition to most dips, a delicious complement to meaty grills, kebabs and fish, and a punchy addition to salads. The vinegar and lemon juice combined with the sumac turn the onions into a striking deep pink, so it not only tastes great, but also looks the part!

MAKES: 1 small jar

4 tbsp white wine vinegar

1 tsp salt

1 tsp soft brown sugar

180ml/6fl oz/¾ cup boiling water

6 tbsp lemon juice

1 tsp sumac

2 tsp pink peppercorns

1 small or medium red onion, thinly sliced

See page 208

First, sterilize the jar you want to use (see page 210).

In a medium bowl, mix the vinegar, salt, sugar and boiling water until the sugar and salt completely dissolve.

Add the lemon juice, sumac and pink peppercorns.

Place the sliced onion in the sterilized jar and pour the pickling liquid on top until the onions are completely covered. Leave to cool.

Once the liquid is completely cool, seal with the lid and place the jar in the refrigerator for at least 2 hours to pickle before serving. Keep in the refrigerator for up to 2 weeks.

Cauliflower Florets Pickle with Turmeric

Particularly lovely with barbecued meats, these bright-yellow cauliflower florets will add a pickled punch to anything you eat. Wait a couple of days and the colour will become incredibly fluorescent, allowing you to decorate dishes while adding some zest. The quantities suggested are for a medium jar; for a large one, double the quantities.

75ml/2½fl oz/⅓ cup white wine vinegar

300ml/10½fl oz/1¼ cups water

10g/¼oz caster/granulated sugar

1 tsp salt

1 small clove garlic, peeled but left whole

2 tsp ground turmeric

1 tbsp coriander seeds

1 small or ½ large cauliflower, broken into small florets

See page 208

First, sterilize the jar you want to use. Wash the jar in hot, soapy water, rinse well and leave to drip dry. Place in a preheated oven at 160°C/320°F/Gas 2½ for 15 minutes. Leave to cool. When handling, only hold from the outside to keep it sterilized.

In a large bowl, whisk the vinegar, water, sugar and salt together until the sugar and salt completely dissolve. Add the garlic, turmeric and coriander seeds and stir again.

Place the cauliflower florets in the sterilized jar and pour the vinegar solution on top to completely cover the cauliflower. Seal with the lid and keep in the refrigerator for up to 2 weeks. Leave for a couple of days before eating.

Mini Cucumber Pickle with Dill & Garlic

This is my favourite pickle of all! It reminds me of my student life, when I would devour a whole jar in an instant. It was and still is my ultimate snack. It takes about a week for the cucumbers to pickle: you can tell they're ready when their colour changes from bright green to a deeper olive shade. The smaller the cucumbers, the better and crunchier they taste.

MAKES: 1 medium jar

75ml/2½fl oz/⅓ cup white
  wine vinegar

300ml/10½fl oz/1¼ cups water

2 tsp caster/granulated sugar

1 tsp salt

1 tbsp coriander seeds

4 garlic cloves, peeled but
  left whole

6–7 mini cucumbers

Small bunch of dill, washed

See page 209

Sterilize the jar you want to use (see page 210).

In a large bowl, whisk the vinegar, water, sugar and salt together until the sugar and salt completely dissolve. Add the coriander seeds and garlic.

Place the cucumbers in the sterilized jar so they fit snugly, then pour the liquid on top until it covers the cucumbers completely. Push the dill down the sides.

Seal with the lid and keep in the refrigerator. It will be ready in about a week and will last for up to 2 weeks.

Acknowledgements

Thank you to all the wonderful people that I had the pleasure of working with throughout this entire process. In particular, thank you to Etan Ilfeld and the Watkins Media group for approaching me, having a shared vision and being incredible partners. To Ella Chappell, my senior commissioning editor, for being my first port of call; calm, professional and a joy to work with. To Fra Corsini, for her lovely designs. To Karen Smith, for her fabulous aesthetic eye when designing the book – thank you for getting me and being so accommodating all the way to the end. To our food stylist, Bianca Nice, whose efficiency and experience helped bring the dishes to life, alongside Gareth Morgans who captured them through his lens so beautifully and was such a pleasure to work with. Thank you to Charlotte Whatcott and Becci Hutchings for your expertise and for making sure everything ran smoothly, as well as Hannah Wilkinson, for her elegant and tasteful props. I would work with you all again in a heartbeat.

Special thanks to Claudia Roden for your kind endorsement; you have always been my cooking idol. It is a dream come true.

To our Delamina team: thank you for your unwavering support and for taking such pride for what we've achieved together; for always looking after the business so passionately and attentively – you really are a part of our extended family. Special thanks to my two head chefs: to Cristiano, for really understanding what Amir and I wanted to create at Delamina, your uncompromising passion for food and technical know-how, and for always being readily available to have food chats with me. To Fabio, for taking amazing care of the kitchen and bringing an infectious cheerfulness, can-do attitude, and a meticulous management style.

ABOVE: With mum and dad

RIGHT: Cooking with dad

BELOW: Picking dates in my grandmother's kibbutz

To our amazing managers, Katya, Rosanna and Marco: thank you for the love and care you have for our Delaminas and for being such great ambassadors of our restaurants.

I want to thank my mum for instilling in me a strong appreciation and awareness for the nutritional aspects of the food I ate from a young age, and for your moral compass that guides me to this day. Thank you, Dad, for showing me how to be confident in the kitchen, allowing me to trust my instincts and be creative, and for setting an example on how to combine drive with poise and dignity. Most of all, I'm grateful to you both for your unequivocal love and belief in me, and in everything I do.

Thank you to my sisters, for our special bond, support, and deep love and understanding we have for each other, no matter where we are in the world.

A huge thank you to my son, Eldar, for being fully engaged in every step of this journey. Thank you for taking a big chunk of your time to edit my work, and doing so with a meticulous eye, passion and excitement. You skilfully managed to keep my voice while making it sound better. Thank you for your creativity, encouragement, methodological thinking and attention to details throughout this process. Your input was invaluable and I'm forever grateful for sharing this experience. It was a joy working with you.

Thank you to my daughter Daniella for your sensitivity throughout this time. For your compassion, intuition, patience and moral support. For always being aware of my wellbeing, and for making me food when I forgot to eat. For your constructive criticism, considered point of view and aesthetic input. Your encouragement and belief in me was empowering.

Lunch with Eldar

Cooking with Daniella

Last, but by no means least: my husband Amir. None of this would have happened if it weren't for your tremendous energy, healthy instincts and business skills that created our Delaminas. Thank you for being my rock, my best friend and business partner. For your support and input throughout this journey, for our late-night book chats and edits, and for enabling me to have some headspace to focus on this book. For being proud, and always happy to be the first taster of any dish I make!

INDEX